RANDOM HOUSE
WEBSTER'S

pocket
power
vocabulary

RANDOM HOUSE
WEBSTER'S

pocket
power
vocabulary

LAURIE ROZAKIS, PH.D.

RANDOM HOUSE
REFERENCE

NEW YORK TORONTO LONDON SYDNEY AUCKLAND

Editorial review and development: Sharon Goldstein, Sol Steinmetz, Carole Cooke, Anne D. Steinhardt; *pronunciations:* Alice Kovac Somoroff; *indexing:* J. Mauricio Sola; *book design and composition:* The Sarabande Press.

Library of Congress Cataloging-in-Publication Data is available.

New York   Toronto   London   Sydney   Auckland

CONTENTS

1. Building a Powerful Vocabulary   3

2. Pronunciation   12

3. Using Prefixes   23

4. Using Suffixes   34

5. Root Power I   42

6. Root Power II   98

7. Word Histories I   156

8. Word Histories II   212

9. Imported Words   263

10. Special Words   284

11. Puzzles   294

     Index of Vocabulary Words   321

     Index of Roots, Prefixes, Suffixes, and Special Words   337

Power
Vocabulary

1. BUILDING A POWERFUL VOCABULARY

INTRODUCTION

Increasingly, the person with a powerful vocabulary has a better chance of success in all walks of life. Numerous studies have demonstrated that successful business executives share a common ability to use words to their advantage.

Why is a strong vocabulary such an important asset? Words are the building blocks of thought. They are the means by which we understand the ideas of others and express our own opinions. It is only logical then that people who know how to use words concisely and accurately find it easier to achieve their aims.

In fact, formal education has less relationship to vocabulary achievement than you might expect, indicating that people *can* improve their word power on their own. This book will show you how to expand and improve your vocabulary in *just ten minutes a day!*

HOW TO USE THIS BOOK

Each of the lessons in this book is designed to take ten minutes to complete. Do one lesson a day. Work in order beginning with Chapter 1 because the lessons build on each other. Follow these three easy steps:

Step 1: Time

Begin by setting aside a block of ten minutes a day. Don't split your time into two five-minute segments—set aside one ten-minute period every day. Consider using ten minutes in the early morning before you begin your regular activities. Or you might want to use ten minutes on the bus, subway, or train or ten minutes during a work break. Maybe right after dinner is a convenient time for you. Whatever time you select, make it *your* time—carve it in granite! To make your work even easier, try to set aside the same time every day. You'll be surprised at how quickly your vocabulary builds.

Step 2: Place

Now, find a place where you can work undisturbed. If you know that you have difficulty tuning out the distractions of public transportation or the office lunchroom, try to study at home. Perhaps you have the ability to completely ignore extraneous chatter or music and so can concentrate in the middle of the family room or in a crowded cafeteria. Wherever you decide to study, try to settle in the same place every day. In this way, you'll set to work more quickly, concentrate better, and succeed sooner.

Step 3: Method

Ten minutes a day is all it takes to build a powerful vocabulary. To help you get into the rhythm of working in ten-minute segments, set your alarm or kitchen timer for ten minutes. When you hear the buzzer, you'll know that you've spent ten minutes on your vocabulary. Soon you'll be able to pace yourself without the timer.

Remember that you *can* succeed, because you've got what it takes. Stick with the book, and in just a few short weeks, you'll be well on your way to the effective, powerful vocabulary you want and need.

TEST YOUR VOCABULARY

How Good Is Your Vocabulary?

To see how your vocabulary measures up to that of other people, take the following tests. As you go through each test, put a check mark next to any word you don't know. After you complete each test, go back and see which of your choices proved correct. Then take a minute to study the words you missed.

The first test consists of twenty-five phrases, each containing an italicized word. Circle the correct response. This test has no time limit.

1. a *lenient* supervisor
   a. short   c. inflexible
   b. not strict   d. shrewd

2. an *audacious* endeavor
   a. foolish   c. expensive
   b. serious   d. bold

3. a *latent* talent
   a. apparent   c. present but not
                          apparent
   b. valuable   d. useless

4. a *gaudy* dress
   a. expensive   c. flattering
   b. deep green   d. showy

5. a *disheveled* person
   a. useless   c. miserable
   b. untidy   d. vicious

6. *feign* illness
   a. suffer   c. die from
   b. pretend   d. enjoy

7. an *agile* child
   a. intelligent   c. neglected
   b. nimble   d. annoying

8. a *somber* night
   a. dismal   c. lively
   b. expensive   d. disastrous

9. a *prosaic* event
   a. extraordinary   c. commonplace
   b. irregular   d. pretty

10. a *vivacious* person
    a. annoying   c. vicious
    b. dismal   d. spirited

11. a *baffling* situation
    a. puzzling   c. easy
    b. obvious   d. old

12. a *hiatus* in the schedule
    a. continuation   c. gap
    b. uniformity   d. beginning

13. a *lackluster* report
    a. enthusiastic   c. dull
    b. praiseworthy   d. wordy

14. a *prevalent* condition
    a. adult   c. previous
    b. widespread   d. fatal

15. a *loquacious* person
    a. talkative   c. laconic
    b. cutthroat   d. enthusiastic

16. an *anonymous* victim
    a. willing   c. not known or named
    b. known   d. foreign

17. a *vicarious* thrill
    a. incomplete   c. spoiled
    b. triumphant   d. indirect

18. a *languid* feeling
    a. nervous   c. fatigued
    b. energetic   d. robust

19. *vernacular* language
    a. ordinary   c. formal
    b. elevated   d. informal

20. a religious *icon*
    a. gesture   c. ritual
    b. picture   d. structure

21. *inclement* weather
    a. fair   c. foul
    b. unexpected   d. disturbing

22. a *cavalier* attitude
    a. pleasant
    b. dramatic
    c. considerate
    d. arrogant
23. a *caustic* remark
    a. wise
    b. biting
    c. prudent
    d. complimentary
24. a timely *caveat*
    a. bargain
    b. purchase
    c. warning
    d. movement
25. an *ominous* situation
    a. pleasant
    b. rigid
    c. obvious
    d. threatening

Answers: 1. b   2. d   3. c   4. d   5. b
6. b   7. b   8. a   9. c   10. d   11. a
12. c   13. c   14. b   15. a   16. c   17. d
18. c   19. a   20. b   21. c   22. d   23. b
24. c   25. d

Refer to the following chart to score your results:

0–6 correct	Below average
7–13 correct	Average
14–20 correct	Above average
21–25 correct	Superior

The following three tests evaluate whether you have an average, good, or excellent vocabulary. The tests have no time limit.

Test for an Average Vocabulary

If you have an average vocabulary, you should be able to match the two columns below correctly. Write your answer in the space provided. Nearly three quarters of the adults tested knew all these words.

1. IMMINENT	a. cleanse	_____
2. FLUSTER	b. flashy	_____
3. RIGID	c. confuse	_____
4. PURGE	d. restore	_____
5. REHABILITATE	e. hinder	_____
6. LATENT	f. pretend	_____
7. GAUDY	g. stiff	_____
8. FEIGN	h. coax	_____
9. CAJOLE	i. hidden	_____
10. IMPEDE	j. at hand	_____

Answers: 1. j   2. c   3. g   4. a   5. d
6. i   7. b   8. f   9. h   10. e

Test for a Good Vocabulary

Only half the adults tested got all of the following words correct. See how well *you* can do! Write S if the word in the second column is similar in meaning to the word in the first column or O if it is opposite.

		S or O
1. MYRIAD	few	_____
2. PANACEA	cure-all	_____

			S or O
3.	OPULENT	spare	_____
4.	ESCHEW	shun	_____
5.	NEFARIOUS	wicked	_____
6.	INCARCERATE	imprison	_____
7.	AMELIORATE	make worse	_____
8.	CANDOR	hypocrisy	_____
9.	TACITURN	talkative	_____
10.	VERBOSE	wordy	_____

Answers: 1. O   2. S   3. O   4. S   5. S
6. S   7. O   8. O   9. O   10. S

Test for an Excellent Vocabulary

Fewer than one quarter of the adults tested got all of the following words correct. In the space provided, write T if the definition is true or F if it is false.

	T or F
1. *Obsequiousness* is a sign of pride.	_____
2. *Parsimonious* people are extravagant.	_____
3. Recycling is an *exigency* of the moment.	_____
4. The hawk is a *predatory* bird.	_____
5. An *aquiline* nose is straight.	_____
6. A *covert* plan is out in the open.	_____
7. It is hard to explain things to an *obtuse* person.	_____
8. Someone with *catholic* views is narrow-minded.	_____

9. A large debt *obviates* financial
   worries.   _____
10. *Erudite* people are well-read.   _____

Answers: 1. F   2. F   3. T   4. T   5. F
6. F   7. T   8. F   9. F   10. T

2. PRONUNCIATION

Obviously, knowing the meaning of a word is only half the battle: you also have to know how to pronounce it. The best way to learn how to pronounce new words is by using a dictionary. Get a reputable, reliable desk or pocket dictionary. The dictionary will improve your public speaking as well as your writing and comprehension. It is the best source for the words you need to get you where you want to go. The following pronunciation key, taken by permission from the *Random House Webster's College Dictionary*, will help you master the material in this book.

Pronunciation Key

act, cāpe, dâre, pärt; set, ēven; if, īce; ox, nō, fôr, oil, bŏŏk, bōōt, out; up, ûrge; child; sing; shoe; thin, that; zh in *treasure.* ə = *a* in *alone, e* in *item, i* in *easily, o* in *gallop, u* in *circus;* ᵊ in *fire* (fīᵊr), *hour* (ouᵊr). N=nasal pronunciation of the previous vowel.

LESSON 1 🕐

TEST YOUR PRONUNCIATION

How Good Is Your Pronunciation?

Let's see how you pronounce some fairly difficult words. As you work through each test, put a check mark next to any word whose pronunciation you don't know. After you finish each test, go back and see which of your choices were right. (Some words have alternate pronunciations.) Finally, take a few minutes to study the words you missed.

The following test contains twenty words. See how many you can pronounce correctly. There is no time limit.

Test 1: Pronunciation

1. badinage
2. salubrious
3. apocryphal
4. putsch
5. effeminacy
6. effusive
7. mandible
8. raison d'être
9. amblyopia
10. dacha
11. exegesis
12. dishabille
13. élan
14. febrile
15. gamut
16. obsequious
17. jejune
18. ribald
19. gecko
20. wizened

Answers: To satisfy your curiosity, here are the definitions as well as the pronunciations. To rank yourself against others, refer to the chart at the end of this section.

If you are not familiar with the pronunciation symbols, refer to the key above.

1. **badinage** (bad′n äzh′, bad′n ij) light, playful banter or raillery
2. **salubrious** (sə lōō′brē əs) favorable to or promoting health; healthful
3. **apocryphal** (ə pok′rə fəl) of doubtful authenticity; false
4. **putsch** (pŏŏch) a plot to overthrow a government
5. **effeminacy** (i fem′ə nə sē) the quality of being soft or delicate to an unmanly degree in traits, tastes, habits, etc.
6. **effusive** (i fyōō′siv) unduly demonstrative; lacking reserve
7. **mandible** (man′də bəl) the bone of the lower jaw
8. **raison d'être** (rā′zōn de′trə) reason or justification for being or existing
9. **amblyopia** (am′blē ō′pē ə) dimness of sight, without an apparent organic cause
10. **dacha** (dä′chə) a Russian country house or villa
11. **exegesis** (ek′si jē′sis) a critical explanation or interpretation, especially of Scripture
12. **dishabille** (dis′ə bēl′) the state of being carelessly or partly dressed; a state of disarray or disorder
13. **élan** (ā län′) dash; impetuous ardor

14. **febrile** (fē′brəl, feb′rəl) feverish
15. **gamut** (gam′ət) the entire scale or range
16. **obsequious** (əb sē′kwē əs) servile, compliant, or deferential
17. **jejune** (ji jōōn′) insipid, dull; childish; deficient or lacking in nutritive value
18. **ribald** (rib′əld) vulgar or indecent in speech; coarsely mocking
19. **gecko** (gek′ō) a harmless nocturnal lizard
20. **wizened** (wiz′ənd) withered; shriveled

Now use this chart to score your results:

0–5 correct	Below average
6–10 correct	Average
11–15 correct	Above average
16–20 correct	Superior

Want to try again? See how many of these twenty words you can pronounce correctly. The test has no time limit.

Test 2: Pronunciation

1. vignette
2. bailiwick
3. juvenilia
4. baroque
5. flaccid
6. cupidity
7. ghee
8. sententious
9. zealous
10. ragout
11. blasé
12. cabochon
13. loath
14. quotidian
15. obdurate
16. cache
17. jocund
18. cabriolet
19. escutcheon
20. penuche

Answers: To rank yourself against others, refer to the chart at the end of this section.

1. **vignette** (vin yet′) a short, graceful literary sketch; a decorative design or small illustration used on the title page of a book or at the beginning or end of a chapter

2. **bailiwick** (bā′lə wik′) a person's area of skill, knowledge, or training; the district within which a bailiff has jurisdiction

3. **juvenilia** (jōō′və nil′ē ə) works, especially writings, produced in youth

4. **baroque** (bə rōk′) extravagantly ornamented; ornate; designating a style of art or music of the 17th–18th century

5. **flaccid** (flak′sid) soft and limp; flabby

6. **cupidity** (kyōō pid′i tē) eager or inordinate desire, especially for wealth; greed or avarice

7. **ghee** (gē) liquid butter made from the milk of cows and buffalos and clarified by boiling, used in Indian cooking

8. **sententious** (sen ten′shəs) given to excessive moralizing; self-righteous; abounding in pithy aphorisms or maxims, as a book

9. **zealous** (zel′əs) ardently active or devoted

10. **ragout** (ra gōō′) a highly seasoned stew of meat or fish

11. **blasé** (blä zā′) indifferent to or bored with life or a particular activity

12. **cabochon** (kab′ə shon′) a precious stone of convex hemispherical or oval form, polished but not cut into facets
13. **loath** (lōth, lōth) unwilling; reluctant
14. **quotidian** (kwō tid′ē ən) daily; everyday; ordinary
15. **obdurate** (ob′doo rit, -dyoo-) unmoved by persuasion, pity, or tender feelings; unyielding
16. **cache** (kash) a hiding place
17. **jocund** (jok′ənd) cheerful; merry
18. **cabriolet** (kab′rē ə lā′) a light, two-wheeled one-horse carriage
19. **escutcheon** (i skuch′ən) a shield or shieldlike surface on which a coat of arms is depicted
20. **penuche** (pə noo′chē) a candy made of brown sugar, butter, and milk, usually with nuts

Refer to the following chart to score your results:

0–6 correct	Below average
7–13 correct	Average
14–20 correct	Above average
21–25 correct	Superior

LESSON 2 🕐

Here are several more pronunciation quizzes to provide you with additional practice.

Test 1: Pronunciation

1. dybbuk	11. insouciance
2. hauteur	12. folderol
3. nacre	13. cavil
4. sidle	14. macabre
5. toque	15. elision
6. viscid	16. denouement
7. lingua franca	17. parvenu
8. shoji	18. pince-nez
9. guano	19. alopecia
10. apropos	20. chicanery

Answers:

1. **dybbuk** (dib′ək) in Jewish folklore, a demon or the soul of a dead person that enters the body of a living person and controls him or her

2. **hauteur** (hō tûr′) a haughty manner or spirit

3. **nacre** (nā′kər) mother-of-pearl

4. **sidle** (sīd′l) to move sideways

5. **toque** (tōk) a soft, brimless, close-fitting hat for women; a chef's hat; a velvet hat with a narrow, turned-up brim, a full crown, and a plume, worn especially in the sixteenth century

6. **viscid** (vis′id) having a glutinous consistency; sticky

7. **lingua franca** (ling′gwə frang′kə) a language widely used as a means of communi-

cation among speakers of different languages

8. **shoji** (shō′jē) a light screen of translucent paper, used as a sliding door or a room divider in Japanese homes

9. **guano** (gwä′nō) a natural manure composed chiefly of the excrement of sea birds, found especially on islands near the Peruvian coast; bird lime

10. **apropos** (ap′rə pō′) appropriate; timely; to the purpose; opportunely; with reference or regard

11. **insouciance** (in sōō′sē əns) lack of care or concern; indifference

12. **folderol** (fol′də rol′) mere nonsense; foolish talk or ideas

13. **cavil** (kav′əl) to quibble; an irritating or trivial objection

14. **macabre** (mə kä′brə) gruesome; horrible; grim

15. **elision** (i lizh′ən) the omission of a vowel, consonant, or syllable in pronunciation

16. **denouement** (dā′nōō mäN′) the final resolution of a plot, as of a drama or novel; outcome

17. **parvenu** (pär′və nōō′, -nyōō′) a person who has suddenly acquired wealth or importance but lacks the proper social qualifications; upstart

18. **pince-nez** (pans′nā′, pins′-) a pair of eyeglasses held on the face by a spring that pinches the nose

19. **alopecia** (al'ə pē'shē ə, -sē ə) baldness
20. **chicanery** (shi kā'nə rē, chi-) trickery or deception by the use of cunning or clever tricks

Test 2: Pronunciation

1. façade
2. obeisance
3. gnome
4. diva
5. liaison
6. mauve
7. fiat
8. kiosk
9. chassis
10. omniscient
11. defalcation
12. contumacious
13. heinous
14. emollient
15. gibe
16. ewer
17. hirsute
18. ogle
19. ennui
20. canard

Answers:

1. **façade** (fə säd') the front of a building, especially an imposing or decorative one; a superficial appearance or illusion of something
2. **obeisance** (ō bā'səns, ō bē'-) a movement of the body expressing deep respect or deferential courtesy, as before a superior; a deep bow
3. **gnome** (nōm) one of a legendary species of diminutive creatures, usually described as shriveled little old men, who inhabit the interior of the earth and act as guardians of its treasure; troll; dwarf

4. **diva** (dē′və, -vä) a distinguished female singer; prima donna
5. **liaison** (lē ā′zən, lē′ā zôn′, lē′ə zon′) a contact maintained between units to ensure concerted action; an illicit sexual relationship
6. **mauve** (mōv, môv) pale bluish purple
7. **fiat** (fē′ät, -at; fī′ət, -at) an authoritative decree, sanction, or order
8. **kiosk** (kē′osk, kē osk′) a kind of open pavilion or summerhouse common in Turkey and Iran; a similar structure used as a bandstand, newsstand, etc.
9. **chassis** (chas′ē, -is, shas′ē) the frame, wheels, and machinery of a motor vehicle, on which the body is supported
10. **omniscient** (om nish′ənt) having complete or infinite knowledge, awareness, or understanding; perceiving all things; all-knowing
11. **defalcation** (dē′fal kā′shən, -fôl-) the misappropriation of money held by an official, trustee, or other fiduciary
12. **contumacious** (kon′tōō mā′shəs, -tyōō-) stubbornly perverse or rebellious; obstinately disobedient
13. **heinous** (hā′nəs) hateful; odious
14. **emollient** (i mol′yənt) something that softens or soothes the skin, as a medical substance
15. **gibe** (jīb) to mock, jeer; a caustic remark
16. **ewer** (yōō′ər) a pitcher with a wide spout

17. **hirsute** (hûr′so͞ot,   hûr   so͞ot′) hairy; shaggy
18. **ogle** (ō′gəl) to look at amorously, flirtatiously, or impertinently
19. **ennui** (än wē′) weariness and discontent resulting from satiety or lack of interest; boredom
20. **canard** (kə närd′) a false story, report, or rumor, usually derogatory

3. USING PREFIXES

A prefix is a letter or group of letters placed at the beginning of a word to change its meaning. Later (Chapters 5 and 6) we will show you how knowing a handful of roots can help you figure out scores of words. Here we will begin by teaching you a few prefixes that can open the door to more powerful words. Here, for example, is a sampling of words that derive from the Latin prefix "circum-," meaning *around*.

Circum- Words

circumambulate	to walk around
circumference	the outer boundary of something
circumfluent	flowing around; encompassing
circumfuse	to surround, as with fluid
circumjacent	lying around; surrounding
circumlocution	a roundabout way of speaking
circumlunar	rotating about the moon
circumnavigate	to sail around
circumpolar	around or near one of the earth's poles
circumrotate	to rotate like a wheel
circumscribe	to encircle; mark off or delimit; restrict

LESSON 1 🕐

LATIN PREFIXES

Below are ten common Latin prefixes and their variations. Study the chart and examples. Then, to help you remember them, complete the self-tests that follow.

Prefix	Meaning	Variations	Examples
1. ad-	to, toward		adjoin, adverb
		a-	ascribe
		ac-	accede
		af-	affix
		ag-	aggregate
		at-	attempt
2. com-	with, together		commotion
		co-	cohabit, coworker
		col-	collaborate
		con-	concede, conduct
		cor-	correlate, correspond
3. de-	down		depress, deform
4. dis-	away, apart, opposite of	di-	disagree, dishonest
		dif-	divert
			diffuse

Prefix	Meaning	Variations	Examples
5. ex-	out		exchange, excavate
		e-	elongate, evaporate
		ec-	eccentric
		ef-	effluent, effuse
6. in-	in, into		inscribe, inhabit
		il-	illuminate
		im-	import, impart
		ir-	irradiate
7. in-	not		inflexible, indecent
		ig-	ignoble
		il-	illiterate, illegal
		im-	immodest, impatient
		ir-	irregular
8. pre-	before		premature
9. pro-	forward		proclaim
10. re-	again, back		recover, return

Test 1: Applying Latin Prefixes

Each of the following phrases contains an italicized word. Based on the meaning of its prefix, select the closest synonym. Circle the correct response.

1. *adjudicate* the matter
   a. sit in judgment on   c. argue
   b. throw out   d. adjust

2. an *illicit* affair
   a. public   c. unlawful
   b. external   d. renewed

3. an important *confederation*
   a. visit   c. church
   b. return   d. alliance

4. *prolong* a speech
   a. shorten   c. extend
   b. dictate   d. preserve

5. an *accredited* school
   a. second-rate   c. undesirable
   b. authorized   d. separated

6. valuable *collateral*
   a. security   c. opinions
   b. comments   d. animals

7. *ascribe* the phrase to
   a. write   c. scribble
   b. scrawl   d. credit

8. *imbibe* too freely
   a. speak   c. travel
   b. drink   d. laugh

9. *precursor* of greater things
   a. banner   c. forerunner
   b. detractor   d. hope

10. *compress* metal
    a. help   c. squeeze
    b. coat   d. buff

Answers: 1. a   2. c   3. d   4. c   5. b
6. a   7. d   8. b   9. c   10. c

Test 2: Defining Words

Based on the meaning of its prefix, define each of the following words.

1. accord _____
2. irradiate _____
3. predestination _____
4. reincarnation _____
5. convolution _____
6. invoke _____
7. cohabit _____
8. irrelevant _____
9. irreducible _____
10. excommunicate _____

Suggested Answers: 1. agreement 2. illuminate 3. fate; destiny 4. rebirth; resurrection 5. a rolled up or coiled condition 6. to request or call forth 7. to live together as husband and wife 8. not relevant 9. incapable of being reduced 10. to exclude from communion

LESSON 2 🕐

GREEK PREFIXES

Below are five common Greek prefixes and their variations. Study the chart and examples. Then, to help you remember the prefixes, complete the self-tests that follow.

Prefix	Meaning	Variations	Examples
1. a-	not, without		atypical, asexual
		an-	anarchy
2. apo-	off, away		apology, apostrophe
3. epi-	beside, upon		epigraph, epidermis
		ep-	epoch
4. para-	beside		paragraph, paraphrase
5. syn-	together, with		synthesis, synonym
		syl-	syllable, syllogism
		sym-	symbiosis, symphony

Test 1: Applying Greek Prefixes

Each of the following phrases contains an italicized word. Based on the meaning of its prefix select the closest synonym. Circle your response

Formed from

1. a new *synagogue*
   a. combination c. house of worship
   b. sentence   d. building

Greek "syn-" + "-agogos," *bringer, gatherer*

2. the true *apogee*
a. limit of endurance	c. closest point of an orbit	Greek "apo-" + "ge," *earth*
b. insult	d. farthest point of an orbit	

3. the fifth annual *synod*
a. church council	c. house-cleaning	Greek "syn-" + "hodos,"
b. religious holiday	d. painting	*way*

4. the sad *episode*
a. incident	c. death	Greek "epi-" + "hodos,"
b. anecdote	d. accident	*way*

5. the witty *epigram*
a. television show	c. saying	Greek "epi-" + "gramma,"
b. radio broadcast	d. song	*something written*

6. guilty of *apostasy*
a. murder	c. an unnamed crime	Greek "apo-" + "stasis,"
b. desertion	d. abandonment of religious faith	*standing*

7. *aseptic* ointment
a. free from germs	c. expensive	Greek "a-" + "septos,"
b. effective	d. greasy	*rotted*

8. clear and effective *syntax*   **Formed from:**
   - a. treatment   c. speech   Greek "syn-"
   - b. word   d. magazine   + "taxis,"
     arrangement   article   *order*

9. injured *epidermis*
   - a. leg ligament   c. skin   Greek "epi-"
   - b. elbow   d. shinbone   + "dermis,"
           skin

10. a cutting *epithet*
    - a. weapon   c. knife   Greek "epi-"
    - b. funeral   d. descriptive   + "theton,"
      oration   word   *placed*

Answers: 1. c   2. d   3. a   4. a   5. c
6. d   7. a   8. b   9. c   10. d

Test 2: Matching Synonyms

Based on your knowledge of Greek prefixes, match each of the numbered words with the closest synonym. Write your answer in the space provided.

1. SYLLOGISM	a. running beside	_____
2. PARALEGAL	b. climax; highest point	_____
3. ANONYMOUS	c. bottomless hole	_____
4. ANESTHETIC	d. one sent out; messenger	_____
5. APOSTLE	e. logical argument	_____
6. PARALLEL	f. doubting God's existence	_____

7. APOCRYPHAL	g. attorney's assistant _____
8. APOGEE	h. false; spurious _____
9. AGNOSTIC	i. causing loss of feeling _____
10. ABYSS	j. nameless _____

Answers: 1. e 2. g 3. j 4. i 5. d
6. a 7. h 8. b 9. f 10. c

LESSON 3 🕐

ANGLO-SAXON PREFIXES

Below are the five most common Anglo-Saxon prefixes and their variations. Study the chart and examples. Then, to help you remember the prefixes, complete the self-tests that follow.

Prefix	Meaning	Examples
a-	on, to, at, by	ablaze, afoot
be-	over, around	bespeak, besiege
mis-	wrong, badly	mistake, misspell
over-	beyond, above	overreach, overawe
un-	not	unwilling, unethical

Test 1: Applying Anglo-Saxon Prefixes

Each of the following phrases contains an italicized word. Based on the meaning of its prefix, select the closest synonym. Circle your response.

1. a *miscarriage* of justice
   - a. instance
   - b. hero
   - c. failure
   - d. example

2. *beseech* movingly
   a. implore   c. evoke
   b. search   d. refuse

3. walking two *abreast*
   a. together   c. back to back
   b. side by side   d. in tandem

4. *bestowed* on us
   a. hurled   c. dependent
   b. smashed   d. presented

5. an unfortunate *misalliance*
   a. treaty   c. bad deal
   b. conversation   d. improper marriage

6. an *overwrought* patient
   a. highly emotional   c. very restrained
   b. extremely ill   d. overmedicated

7. an *unkempt* look
   a. funny   c. ugly
   b. messy   d. pretty

8. an embarrassing *miscue*
   a. joke   c. step
   b. anecdote   d. error

9. *bedaub* with clay
   a. sculpt   c. smear
   b. present   d. create

10. *bemoan* his situation
    a. celebrate   c. lament
    b. share   d. hide

Answers: 1. c   2. a   3. b   4. d   5. d
6. a   7. b   8. d   9. c   10. c

Test 2: Matching Synonyms

Based on your knowledge of Anglo-Saxon pre-fixes, match each of the numbered words with the closest synonym. Write your answer in the space provided.

1. UNFEIGNED   a. conquer   _____
2. MISBEGOTTEN   b. right on the mark   _____
3. BEGUILE   c. too fervent   _____
4. MISCARRIAGE   d. envy; resent   _____
5. BEMUSE   e. sincere; genuine   _____
6. MISHAP   f. accident   _____
7. OVERCOME   g. illegitimate   _____
8. BEGRUDGE   h. mislead   _____
9. UNERRING   i. bewilder   _____
10. OVERZEALOUS   j. spontaneous abortion   _____

Answers: 1. e   2. g   3. h   4. j   5. i
6. f   7. a   8. d   9. b   10. c

4. Using Suffixes

A suffix is a letter or group of letters placed at the end of a word to change its grammatical function, tense, or meaning. Suffixes can be used to create a verb from a noun or adjective or an adjective from a verb, for example. They can change a word's tense as well; "-ed" can make a present-tense verb into a past participle, for instance. They can even change a word's meaning; the suffix "-ette," for example, can make a word into its diminutive: "kitchen" into "kitchenette."

Just as recognizing a small number of prefixes can help you figure out many unfamiliar words, so knowing a few common suffixes can help you build a more powerful vocabulary.

LESSON 1 🕐

TEN POWERFUL SUFFIXES

Below are ten useful suffixes. Read through the chart and examples. To reinforce your study, complete the self-tests that follow.

Suffix	Meaning	Variations	Examples
1. -ate	to make		alienate, regulate
		marked by	passionate, affectionate

Suffix	Meaning	Variations	Examples
2. -en	to make		weaken, moisten
3. -ism	the quality or practice of		absolutism, baptism
4. -ation	the act or condition of		allegation, affirmation
		-ition	recognition
		-tion	commotion
5. -ty	the state of		modesty
		-ity	security
6. -er	one that does or deals with		worker, teacher
		-ar	scholar
		-ier	furrier
		-or	bettor
7. -an	one that does or deals with		comedian, historian
8. -al	resembling or pertaining to		natural, accidental
9. -ous	full of		perilous
		-ious	gracious, vicious
10. -able	capable of being		lovable, affordable
		-ible	reversible

Test 1: Applying Suffixes

Each of the following phrases contains an italicized word. Based on the meaning of its suffix
select the closest synonym. Circle your response

1. *combustible* rubbish
   a. unbreakable   c. affordable
   b. able to burst   d. flammable

2. *pastoral* scenes
   a. clerical   c. rural
   b. attractive d. homely

3. a *partisan* of the rebellion
   a. flag   c. sign
   b. supporter   d. result

4. a *palatial* home
   a. magnificent c. formal
   b. modest   d. enjoyable

5. the *collegiate* atmosphere
   a. churchlike c. cooperative
   b. friendly   d. academic

6. *assiduity* in studies
   a. alacrity   c. diligence
   b. cleverness d. laziness

7. a country of *pedestrians*
   a. scholars   c. shopkeepers
   b. walkers   d. students

8. an *abstemious* eater
   a. aloof   c. absent-minded
   b. idle   d. sparing

9. *perilous* practices
   a. commonplace   c. dangerous
   b. rare   d. useless
10. *deleterious* effects
   a. good   c. bad
   b. neutral   d. delightful

Answers: 1. d   2. c   3. b   4. a   5. d
6. c   7. b   8. d   9. c   10. c

Test 2: Matching Synonyms

Based on your knowledge of suffixes, match each of the numbered words with the closest synonym. If in doubt, refer to the root word that follows each numbered word.

1. CULPABLE   a. blameworthy
   (Root word: Latin
   "culpa," *blame*)
2. PARITY   b. injurious
   (Root word: Latin
   "par," *equal*)
3. AMENABLE   c. everlasting
   (Root word: French
   "amener," *to lead to*)
4. MENDACIOUS   d. reversion to type
   (Root word: Latin
   "mendax," *dishonest*)

5. SEMPITERNAL   e. equality
   (Root word: Latin
   "semper," *always*)

6. NIHILISM   f. to chastise; censure
   (Root word: Latin
   "nihil," *nothing*)

7. ATAVISM   g. willing
   (Root word: Latin
   "atavus," *remote*)

8. FEALTY   h. total rejection of law
   (Root word: French
   "fealté," *fidelity*)

9. CASTIGATE   i. lying; false
   (Root word: Latin
   "castus," *chaste*)

10. NOXIOUS   j. faithfulness
   (Root word: Latin
   "noxa," *harm*)

Answers: 1. a   2. e   3. g   4. i   5. c
6. h   7. d   8. j   9. f   10. b

LESSON 2 🕐

TEN ADDITIONAL POWERFUL SUFFIXES

The following ten suffixes will help you understand countless additional words. After you read through the suffixes and their definitions, complete the two self-tests at the end of the lesson.

Suffix	Meaning	Examples
1. -esque	in the manner of; like	Lincolnesque
2. -aceous	resembling or having	carbonaceous
3. -ic	associated with	democratic
4. -age	act or process of; quantity or measure	marriage, coverage; footage
5. -itis	inflammation	tonsillitis
6. -ish	similar to; like a	foolish; babyish
7. -less	without	guiltless; helpless
8. -ship	occupation or skill; condition of being	authorship, penmanship; friendship
9. -ian	a person who is, does, or participates in	comedian
10. -ferous	bearing or conveying	odoriferous

Test 1: Matching Synonyms

Based on your knowledge of suffixes, match each of the numbered words with its closest synonym. Write your answer in the space provided.

1. WASPISH	a. inattentive, sloppy	_____
2. FELLOWSHIP	b. egotistic	_____
3. ANGELIC	c. distance	_____
4. MILEAGE	d. huge	_____

5. PICTURESQUE	e. eternal	_____
6. CURVACEOUS	f. irritable	_____
7. TITANIC	g. voluptuous	_____
8. CARELESS	h. companionship	_____
9. SELFISH	i. innocent	_____
10. TIMELESS	j. colorful	_____

Answers: 1. f   2. h   3. i   4. c   5. j
6. g   7. d   8. a   9. b   10. e

Test 2: Applying Suffixes

Each of the following phrases contains an italicized word. Based on the meaning of its suffix, select the closest synonym. If in doubt, refer to the root word listed in the right-hand column. Circle your response.

Root Word

1. *auriferous* mineral

| a. containing gold | c. having an odor | Latin "aurum," |
| b. extremely hard | d. very common | *gold* |

2. *conical* shape

| a. humorous; amusing | c. spherical | Greek "konos," |
| b. like a cone | d. rigid | *cone* |

3. suffering from *carditis*

| a. eye infection | c. inflammation of the heart | Greek "kardia," |
| b. a tin ear | d. stiff joints | *heart* |

4. graceful *Romanesque*
   a. architectural style
   b. departure
   c. essay
   d. apology

5. *olivaceous* color
   a. oily
   b. deep green
   c. faded
   d. attractive

6. frightful *carnage*
   a. journey
   b. slaughter
   c. scene
   d. sensuality

   Latin "carnis," *flesh*

7. *satanic* nature
   a. evil
   b. cheerful
   c. shiny
   d. generous

8. admirable *craftsmanship*
   a. display
   b. individual
   c. shop
   d. artfulness

9. *veracious* remarks
   a. vivid
   b. vicious
   c. windy
   d. truthful

   Latin "verus," *true*

10. painful *appendicitis*
    a. news
    b. surgery
    c. inflammation of the appendix
    d. removal of the appendix

Answers: 1. a 2. b 3. c 4. a 5. b
6. b 7. a 8. d 9. d 10. c

5. ROOT POWER I

LATIN AND GREEK ROOTS

One of the quickest and most effective ways to improve your vocabulary is by learning to recognize the most common Latin and Greek roots, since any one of them can help you define a number of English words. Whenever you come upon an unfamiliar word, first check to see if it has a recognizable root. If you know that the Latin root "ami," for example, means *like* or *love,* you can easily figure out that "amiable" means *pleasant, friendly* and "amorous" means *loving.* Even if you cannot define a word exactly, recognizing the root will still give you a general idea of the word's meaning. Remembering that the Greek root "geo" means *earth* would certainly help you define "geophysics" as *the physics of the earth,* but it also might help you figure out that "geocentric" has to do with the center of the earth or with the earth as a center. Begin by studying the following lists of common Latin and Greek roots and representative words.

LESSON 1 🕐

COMMON LATIN ROOTS

Root	Meaning	Example	Definition
ag	act	agent	representative
cad, cas	fall	cadence	rhythmic flow
cap, cept	take, hold	receptacle	container
ced, cess	go	recessive	tending to go back
cid, cis	kill, cut	incision	cut, gash
clud, clus	shut	seclusion	separation from others
cred	believe	credible	believable
cur(r), curs	run	concur	agree (i.e., run together)
fer	bear	odoriferous	yielding an odor
her, hes	cling	adhere	cling, stick
ject	throw	projection	jutting out, protrusion
leg, lect	read	legible	easily readable
pel(l), puls	drive	repulse	repel (i.e., drive back)
pon, posit	put	postpone	defer
port	carry	portable	movable
rupt	break	abrupt	sudden, quick
scrib, script	write	inscription	engraving, writing
sect	cut	dissect	cut apart
sent, sens	feel	sensitive	tender

Root	Meaning	Example	Definition
sequ, secut	follow	sequel	result
spect	look	prospect	outlook, expectation
sta, stat	stand	stable	fixed, firm
tang, tact	touch	tactile	tangible
termin	end	terminate	abolish, end
tract	pull, draw	tractor	vehicle that pulls
ven, vent	come	convene	assemble (i.e. come together)
vert, vers	turn	invert	overturn
vid, vis	see	provident	having foresight
vinc, vict	conquer	invincible	unconquerable
volv, volut	roll, turn	evolve	develop

Test 1: Applying Roots

Each of the following phrases contains an italicized word. Based on the meaning of the root select the closest synonym. Circle your response

1. a *captive* animal
   a. confined
   b. wild
   c. charming
   d. domestic
2. an *inverted* glass
   a. broken
   b. upside-down
   c. returned
   d. drunk from

3. an *abrupt* stop
   a. slow
   b. bad
   c. sudden
   d. harmful

4. a disappointing *sequel*
   a. television show
   b. beginning
   c. movie
   d. follow-up

5. *terminate* the relationship
   a. doubt
   b. intensify
   c. begin
   d. finish

6. an *incredible* story
   a. outlandish
   b. unbelievable
   c. foolish
   d. upsetting

7. a *recessive* trait
   a. dominant
   b. receding
   c. hurtful
   d. missing

8. *illegible* writing
   a. unreadable
   b. graceful
   c. distinct
   d. large

9. a thorough *dissection*
   a. cutting apart
   b. conference
   c. discussion
   d. putting together

10. an *unstable* relationship
    a. new
    b. unsteady
    c. one-sided
    d. unreliable

11. an *odoriferous* cheese
    a. commonplace
    b. brightly colored
    c. malodorous
    d. faded

12. an *invincible* warrior
    a. huge
    b. foreign
    c. defeated
    d. unbeatable

13. the *advent* of summer
    a. departure   c. arrival
    b. middle   d. complaint
14. a *provident* move
    a. prosperous   c. prudent
    b. injudicious   d. hurtful
15. the top-secret *projectile*
    a. missile   c. plan
    b. project   d. meeting

Answers: 1. a 2. b 3. c 4. d 5. d
6. b 7. b 8. a 9. a 10. b 11.
c 12. d 13. c 14. c 15. a

Test 2: True/False

In the space provided, write T if the definition of the numbered word is true or F if it is false.

		T or F
1. ADHERE	cling	_____
2. CADAVER	cavort	_____
3. EVOLVE	develop	_____
4. INCISION	cut	_____
5. CONCURRENT	disjointed	_____
6. RECLUSE	vivacious person	_____
7. INSCRIPTION	story	_____
8. AGENT	deputy	_____
9. TACTILE	tangible	_____
10. REPULSE	repel	_____

Answers: 1. T 2. F 3. T 4. T 5. F
6. F 7. F 8. T 9. T 10. T

LESSON 2 🕐

COMMON GREEK ROOTS

Root	Meaning	Example	Definition
aster, astro	star	asterisk	star-shaped mark
chrom	color	chromatic	pertaining to color
chron, chrono	time	synchronize	occur simultaneously
cosmo	world	cosmopolitan	citizen of the world
dem	people	democracy	government by the people
meter	measure	thermometer	instrument that measures temperature
onym	name, word	pseudonym	a fictitious name
path	feeling	apathy	absence of feeling
phob	fear	claustrophobia	fear of enclosed places
phon	sound	cacophony	harsh, discordant sound
psycho	mind	psychology	science of the mind
soph	wisdom	sophistry	subtle, tricky reasoning

Test 1: True/False

In the space provided, write T if the definition of the numbered word is true or F if it is false.

			T or F
1.	EPIDEMIC	plague	_____
2.	HOMONYM	same-sounding name	_____
3.	CLAUSTROPHOBIA	fear of dogs	_____
4.	CACOPHONY	dissonance	_____
5.	APATHY	enthusiasm	_____
6.	ACCELEROMETER	instrument for measuring acceleration	_____
7.	SYNCHRONIZE	squabble	_____
8.	COSMOPOLITAN	international	_____
9.	SOPHISM	specious argument	_____
10.	CHROMATIC	crisp	_____

Answers: 1. T 2. T 3. F 4. T 5. F
6. T 7. F 8. T 9. T 10. F

Test 2: Applying Greek Roots

Based on the meaning of its root, define each of the following words. If in doubt, check the suggested answers.

1. asteroid _____
2. chromatics _____
3. cosmos _____

4. anonymous _____
5. Anglophobia _____
6. cosmography _____
7. synchronous _____
8. pathetic _____
9. pedometer _____
10. democracy _____
11. phonograph _____
12. demographics _____
13. psychotic _____
14. sophisticated _____
15. cognition _____

Suggested Answers: 1. a small mass that orbits the sun 2. the science of colors 3. universe 4. without any name acknowledged 5. fear of things English 6. the study of the structure of the universe 7. coinciding in time 8. evoking feelings of pity 9. an instrument that measures distance covered in walking 10. government by the people 11. a sound-reproducing machine 12. the statistical data of a population 13. a person who is mentally ill 14. worldly-wise 15. act or fact of knowing

LESSON 3 🕐

"OTHER PLACES, OTHER FACES": AL, ALL, ALTER

An "alibi" is a defense by an accused person who claims to have been elsewhere at the time the offense was committed. The word comes from the Latin root "al," meaning *other*. Outside of law, an alibi often means an excuse, especially to avoid blame.

The Latin roots "al" and "alter," as well as the related Greek root "all" or "allo," all mean *other* or *another*, and form the basis of a number of English words. Below are ten such words. After you study the definitions and practice the pronunciations, complete the quizzes.

1. **alien** (āl′yən, ā′lē ən) a person born in and owing allegiance to a country other than the one in which he or she lives; a nonterrestrial being; foreign or strange.

   Although my neighbor is not an American citizen, he has lived in this country so long he no longer thinks of himself as an alien.

2. **allegory** (al′ə gôr′ē) a representation of an abstract meaning through concrete or material forms; figurative treatment of one subject under the guise of another.

   Nathaniel Hawthorne's short story "Young Goodman Brown" can be read as an allegory of an average person's encounter with sin and temptation.

3. **alias** (ā′lē əs) a false or assumed name, especially as used by a criminal. From the Latin word meaning *otherwise*.

   Many criminals use an alias with the same initials as their real name; Clyde Griffith, for example, took as his alias "Chester Gillett."

4. **alienate** (āl′yə nāt′, ā′lē ə-) to make in-different or hostile. From Latin "alienare," *to make another.*

   Unkempt yards alienate prospective home buyers.

5. **altruism** (al′trōō iz′əm) unselfish concern for the welfare of others.

   Devotion to the poor, sick, and unfortunate of the world shows a person's altruism.

6. **altercation** (ôl′tər kā′shən) a heated or angry dispute; noisy argument or controversy. From Latin "altercari," *to quarrel with another.*

   The collision resulted in an altercation between the two drivers.

7. **inalienable** (in āl′yə nə bəl, -ā′lē ə-) not transferable to another; incapable of being repudiated.

   Freedom of speech is the inalienable right of every American citizen.

8. **allograft** (al′ə graft′) tissue grafted or transplanted to another member of the same species.

   Allografts of vital organs have saved many lives.

9. **allogamy** (ə log′ə mē) cross-fertilization in plants. From "allo-," *other* + "-gamy," *pollination.*

   To ensure allogamy, the farmer set out many different plants close together.

10. **alter ego** (ôl′tər ē′gō) another self; an inseparable friend.

Superman's alter ego, the mild-mannered Clark Kent, is a reporter for the *Daily Planet*.

Test 1: Matching Synonyms

Match each of the numbered words with its closest synonym. Write your answer in the space provided.

1. ALIEN	a. absolute		_____
2. ALIAS	b. cross-fertilization		_____
3. ALTER EGO	c. selflessness, kindness		_____
4. ALLOGAMY	d. best friend		_____
5. ALLEGORY	e. another name		_____
6. INALIENABLE	f. transplant		_____
7. ALTRUISM	g. contention, quarrel		_____
8. ALIENATE	h. symbolic narrative		_____
9. ALLOGRAFT	i. stranger, outcast		_____
10. ALTERCATION	j. turn away, estrange		_____

Answers: 1. i 2. e 3. d 4. b 5. h
6. a 7. c 8. j 9. f 10. g

Test 2: True/False

In the space provided, write T if the definition of the numbered word is true or F if it is false.

		T or F
1. ALIEN	foreign	_____
2. ALIAS	excuse	_____

		T or F
3. ALTER EGO	egotist	_____
4. ALLOGAMY	multiple marriage	_____
5. ALLEGORY	moral story	_____
6. INALIENABLE	without basis in fact	_____
7. ALTRUISM	unselfishness	_____
8. ALIENATE	estrange	_____
9. ALLOGRAFT	illegal money	_____
10. ALTERCATION	dispute	_____

Answers: 1. T 2. F 3. F 4. F 5. T
6. F 7. T 8. T 9. F 10. T

LESSON 4 🕐

"THE BREATH OF LIFE": *ANIMA*

Ancient peoples connected the soul with the breath. They saw that when people died they stopped breathing, and they believed that the soul left the body at the same time. They also believed that when people sneezed, the soul left the body for a moment, so they muttered a hasty blessing to ensure that the soul would return quickly to its rightful place. The Latin root for air or breath, "anima," also means *soul, spirit,* or *mind,* reflecting this belief in a connection between life and breathing. Many English words come from this root.

Below are ten words linked to "anima." After you study the definitions and practice the pronunciations, complete the quizzes.

1. **animation** (an'ə mā'shən) liveliness or vivacity; the act or an instance of animating or enlivening. From Latin "animare," *to give life to.*

   In speech class we learned how to talk with animation to make our presentations more interesting.

2. **animadversion** (an'ə mad vûr'zhən, -shən) criticism; censure. From Latin "animus," *mind, spirit* + "adversio," *attention, warning.*

   The critic's animadversion on the subject of TV shows revealed his bias against popular culture.

3. **animus** (an'ə məs) hostile feeling or attitude.

   The jury's animus toward the defendant was obvious from the jurors' stony faces and stiff posture.

4. **pusillanimous** (pyōō'sə lan'ə məs) lacking courage or resolution; cowardly. From Latin "pusillus," *very small* + "animus," *spirit.*

   He was so pusillanimous that he wouldn't even run away from a bully.

5. **unanimity** (yōō'nə nim'i tē) the state or quality of being in complete agreement; undivided opinion or a consensus. From Latin "unus," *one* + "animus," *mind, spirit.*

   The school board's unanimity on the controversial issue of sex education was all the more surprising in light of their well-known individual differences.

6. **animate** (an'ə māt') to give life or liveliness to; alive.

    Her presence animated the otherwise dull party.

7. **animalcule** (an'ə mal'ky ōōl) a minute or microscopic organism. From Latin "animalis," *living, animal* + "-culum," *tiny thing*.

    The animalcule could not be seen with the naked eye.

8. **magnanimous** (mag nan'ə məs) generous in forgiving an insult or injury; free from petty resentfulness. From Latin "magnus," *large, great* + "animus," *soul*.

    The governor's magnanimous pardon of the offender showed his liberal nature.

9. **inanimate** (in an'ə mit) not alive or lively; lifeless.

    Pinocchio was inanimate, a puppet carved from a block of wood.

10. **animism** (an'ə miz'əm) the belief that natural objects, natural phenomena, and the universe itself possess souls or consciousness.

    Their belief in animism drew them to the woods, where they felt more in touch with nature's spirit.

Test 1: Matching Synonyms

Match each of the numbered words with the closest synonym. Write your answer in the space provided.

1. ANIMADVERSION	a. enliven	_____
2. ANIMUS	b. harmony	_____
3. PUSILLANIMOUS	c. generous	_____
4. UNANIMITY	d. cowardly	_____
5. ANIMATE	e. hostility	_____
6. ANIMALCULE	f. spirit, zest	_____
7. MAGNANIMOUS	g. a censorious remark	_____
8. INANIMATE	h. a belief in spirits	_____
9. ANIMATION	i. a minute organism	_____
10. ANIMISM	j. inert	_____

Answers: 1. g 2. e 3. d 4. b 5. a
6. i 7. c 8. j 9. f 10. h

Test 2: True/False

In the space provided, write T if the definition of the numbered word is true or F if it is false.

		T or F
1. ANIMADVERSION	praise	_____
2. ANIMUS	hostility	_____
3. PUSILLANIMOUS	cowardly	_____
4. UNANIMITY	total agreement	_____

			T or F
5.	ANIMATE	deaden	_____
6.	ANIMALCULE	small soul	_____
7.	MAGNANIMOUS	generous	_____
8.	INANIMATE	living	_____
9.	ANIMATION	liveliness	_____
10.	ANIMISM	love of animals	_____

Answers: 1. F   2. T   3. T   4. T   5. F
6. F   7. T   8. F   9. T   10. F

LESSON 5 🕐

"THE YEAR OF WONDERS": *ANN, ENN*

While certain years are celebrated for great wonders, the first year that was actually designated "The Year of Wonders," *Annus Mirabilis,* was 1666. The English poet, dramatist, and critic John Dryden (1631–1700) enshrined that year as "Annus Mirabilis" in his poem of the same name, which commemorated the English victory over the Dutch and the Great Fire of London. "Annus," meaning *year,* comes from the Latin root "ann," a source of many useful English words. The same root is also written "enn" in the middle of a word.

Below are ten words drawn from this root. After you look over the definitions and practice the pronunciations, complete the quizzes that follow.

1. **per annum** (pər an'əm) by the year; yearly.

   The firm promised to bill the additional interest charges per annum, the invoice to arrive every January.

2. **annual** (an' yōo əl) of, for, or pertaining to a year; yearly.

   The annual enrollment in the high school has increased sharply since the new housing was built.

3. **anniversary** (an'ə vûr'sə rē) the yearly recurrence of the date of a past event, especially the date of a wedding. From Latin "ann(i)," *year* + "vers(us)," *turned* + adjectival suffix "-ary."

   For their twenty-fifth wedding anniversary, the happy couple decided to have dinner at the restaurant where they first met.

4. **biennial** (bī en'ē əl) happening every two years; lasting for two years. From Latin "bi-," *two* + root "enn" + adjectival suffix "-ial."

   My flowering fig tree has a biennial cycle; it blooms every two years.

5. **triennial** (trī en'ē əl) occurring every three years; lasting three years. From Latin "tri-," *three* + root "enn" + adjectival suffix "-ial."

   The university has set up a triennial cycle of promotions to review candidates for advancement.

6. **decennial** (di sen'ē əl) of or for ten years; occurring every ten years. From Latin

"dec(em)," *ten* + root "enn" + adjectival suffix "-ial."

Every ten years, the PTA holds its decennial meeting in the state capital.

7. **centennial** (sen ten′ē əl) of or pertaining to a period of one hundred years; recurring once every hundred years. From Latin "cent(um)," *hundred* + root "enn" + adjectival suffix "-ial."

To celebrate the railroad's centennial anniversary, the town's historical society restored the run-down station so it looked exactly as it did when it was built a hundred years ago.

8. **bicentennial** (bī′sen ten′ē əl) pertaining to or in honor of a two-hundredth anniversary; consisting of or lasting two hundred years.

To advertise its bicentennial festivities next year, the town has adopted the slogan "Celebrating Two Hundred Years of Progress."

9. **millennium** (mi len′ē əm) a period of one thousand years. From Latin "mille," *thousand* + root "enn" + noun suffix "-ium."

Technology advances so rapidly now that we can scarcely imagine what life will be like in the next millennium.

10. **annuity** (ə noō′ i tē, ə nyoō′-) a specified income payable each year or at stated intervals in consideration of a premium paid.

From Latin "ann(uus)," *yearly* + noun suffix "-ity."

The annuity from her late husband's life-insurance policy was barely adequate for the poor widow's needs.

Test 1: Matching Synonyms

Select the best definition for each numbered word. Write your answer in the space provided.

1. BICENTENNIAL	a. every ten years	_____
2. ANNIVERSARY	b. every two years	_____
3. DECENNIAL	c. every two hundred years	_____
4. MILLENNIUM	d. every three years	_____
5. PER ANNUM	e. one thousand years	_____
6. CENTENNIAL	f. fixed payment	_____
7. ANNUITY	g. yearly recurrence of a date	_____
8. TRIENNIAL	h. every hundred years	_____
9. BIENNIAL	i. by the year	_____
10. ANNUAL	j. yearly	_____

Answers: 1. c   2. g   3. a   4. e   5. i
6. h   7. f   8. d   9. b   10. j

Test 2: True/False

In the space provided, write T if the definition of the numbered word is true or F if it is false.

			T or F
1.	ANNUITY	every two hundred years	_____
2.	BICENTENNIAL	every other year	_____
3.	MILLENNIUM	one thousand years	_____
4.	ANNUAL	fixed amount of money	_____
5.	CENTENNIAL	every hundred years	_____
6.	TRIENNIAL	every three years	_____
7.	PER ANNUM	by order	_____
8.	BIENNIAL	every third year	_____
9.	DECENNIAL	every thousand years	_____
10.	ANNIVERSARY	yearly event	_____

Answers: 1. F 2. F 3. T 4. F 5. T
6. T 7. F 8. F 9. F 10. T

LESSON 6 🕐

"MAN OF THE WORLD": *ANTHROPO*

In the early twentieth century, Rudolph Steiner developed an esoteric system of knowledge he called "anthroposophy." Steiner developed the word from the Greek roots "anthropo," meaning *man* or *human*, and "soph," meaning *wisdom*. He defined his philosophy as "the knowledge of the spiritual human being . . . and of everything which the spirit man can perceive in the spiritual world."

We've taken several more words from "anthropo"; below are six of them. After you look over the definitions and practice the pronunciations, complete the quizzes that follow.

1. **anthropoid** (an'thrə poid') resembling humans.

   The child was fascinated by the anthropoid ape on display in the natural history museum.

2. **anthropomorphism** (an'thrə pə môr'fiz-əm) the ascription of human form or attributes to a being or thing not human, such as a deity.

   To speak of the "cruel, crawling foam" is an example of anthropomorphism, for the sea is not cruel.

3. **misanthrope** (mis'ən thrōp', miz'-) a hater of humankind. From Greek "mis(o)," *hate* + "anthropos," *man.*

   In *Gulliver's Travels*, the great misanthrope Jonathan Swift depicts human beings as monstrous savages.

4. **philanthropy** (fi lan'thrə pē) good works; affection for humankind, especially as manifested in donations, as of money, to needy persons or to socially useful purposes. From Greek "phil(o)," *loving* + "anthropos," *man.*

   Thanks to the philanthropy of a wealthy patron, the new hospital wing was fully stocked with the latest equipment.

5. **anthropology** (an'thrə pol'ə jē) the science that deals with the origins, physical and cultural development, racial characteristics,

and social customs and beliefs of humankind.

After the student completed the anthropology course, she visited some of the exotic cultures she had read about.

6. **anthropocentric** (an'thrə pō sen'trik) regarding humans as the central fact of the universe.

Philosophy that views and interprets the universe in terms of human experience and values is anthropocentric.

Test 1: Matching Synonyms

Select the best definition for each numbered word. Write your answer in the space provided.

1. ANTHROPOLOGY a. believing that humans are the center of the universe _____

2. PHILANTHROPY b. one who dislikes people _____

3. ANTHROPO-CENTRIC c. science of humankind's origins, beliefs, and customs _____

4. ANTHROPOID d. personification of inanimate things _____

5. ANTHROPO-MORPHISM e. doing good for people _____

6. MISANTHROPE f. humanlike _____

Answers: 1. c   2. e   3. a   4. f   5. d
6. b

Test 2: True/False

In the space provided, write T if the definition of the numbered word is true or F if it is false.

			T or F
1.	MISANTHROPE	cynic	_____
2.	PHILANTHROPY	goodwill to humankind	_____
3.	ANTHROPO-MORPHISM	insecurity	_____
4.	ANTHROPO-CENTRIC	unselfish	_____
5.	ANTHROPOLOGY	science of flowers	_____
6.	ANTHROPOID	resembling humans	_____

Answers: 1. F   2. T   3. F   4. F   5. F
6. T

LESSON 7 🕐

"KNOW THYSELF": *GNO*

One of the fascinating things about the study of words is the discovery of close relationships between seemingly unrelated words. Because English draws its vocabulary from many sources, it often appropriates foreign words that ultimately derive from the same source as a native

English word. A good example is our word "know," which has its exact equivalent in the Latin and Greek root "gno." Here are eight words from this root. First read through the pronunciations, definitions, and examples. Then complete the quizzes that follow.

1. **cognizant** (kog′nə zənt, kon′ə-) aware. From Latin "cognoscere," *to come to know* ("co-," *together* + "gnoscere," *to know*).

   He was fully cognizant of the difficulty of the mission.

2. **incognito** (in′kog nē′tō, in kog′ni tō′) with one's identity concealed, as under an assumed name. From Latin "incognitus," *not known* ("in-," *not* + "cognitus," *known*).

   The officer from naval intelligence always traveled incognito to avoid any problems with security.

3. **prognosticate** (prog nos′ti kāt′) to forecast from present indications. From Greek "prognostikos," *knowing beforehand* ("pro-," *before* + "(gi)gno(skein)," *to know*).

   The fortuneteller was able to prognosticate with the help of her tea leaves, crystal ball, and a good deal of inside information about her client.

4. **diagnostician** (dī′əg no stish′ən) an expert in determining the nature of diseases. From Greek "diagnosis," *determination* (of a disease) ("dia-," *through* + "(gi)gno(skein)," *to know*).

The diagnostician was able to allay her patient's fears after the x-ray showed that he had suffered only a sprain, not a break.

5. **cognoscenti** (kon'yə shen'tē, kog'nə-) well-informed persons, especially in a particular field, as in the arts. From Italian, ultimately derived from Latin "co-," *together* + "gnoscere," *to know.*

Although the exhibit had only been open one week, the cognoscenti were already proclaiming it the show of the decade.

6. **gnostic** (nos'tik) pertaining to knowledge, especially to the esoteric knowledge taught by an early Christian mystical sect. From Greek "gnostikos," *knowing,* from the root of "(gi)gno(skein)," *to know.*

The gnostic view that everything is knowable is opposed by the agnostic view.

7. **ignoramus** (ig'nə rā'məs, -ram'əs) an extremely uninformed person. From the Latin word meaning *we don't know,* derived from "ignorare," *to not know* ("i(-n-)," *not* + the root of "gno(scere)," *to come to know*).

Only an ignoramus would insist that the earth is flat.

8. **cognition** (kog nish'ən) the act or process of knowing; perception. From Latin "cognitio," derived from "cognoscere," *to come to know* ("co-," *together* + "gnoscere," *to know*).

Cognition is impaired by narcotic drugs.

Test 1: True/False

In the space provided, write T if the definition of the numbered word is true or F if it is false.

			T or F
1.	GNOSTIC	knowing	_____
2.	INCOGNITO	disguised	_____
3.	PROGNOSTICATE	curse	_____
4.	IGNORAMUS	ignorant person	_____
5.	COGNOSCENTI	aromatic herb	_____
6.	COGNITION	perception	_____
7.	DIAGNOSTICIAN	expert mechanic	_____
8.	COGNIZANT	conscious	_____

Answers: 1. F 2. T 3. F 4. T 5. F
6. T 7. F 8. T

Test 2: Defining Words

Define each of the following words.

1. ignoramus _____
2. cognoscenti _____
3. cognition _____
4. incognito _____
5. gnostic _____
6. prognosticate _____
7. diagnostician _____
8. cognizant _____

Suggested Answers: 1. unschooled person
2. those who have a superior knowledge 3. the

act or process of knowing; perception   4. with one's identity concealed 5. pertaining to knowledge 6. to forecast   7. an expert in making diagnoses 8. aware

LESSON 8 🕐

"RULERS AND LEADERS": *ARCH*

In Christian theology, Michael is given the title of "archangel," principal angel and primary opponent of Satan and his horde. The Greek root "arch," meaning *chief, first; rule or ruler*, is the basis of a number of important and useful words.

Below are ten words drawn from this root. Read the definitions and practice the pronunciations. Then study the sample sentences and see if you can use the words in sentences of your own.

1. **archenemy** (ärch'en'ə mē) a chief enemy; Satan.

   In Christian theology, Satan is the archenemy.

2. **patriarch** (pā'trē ärk') the male head of a family or tribe. From Greek "patria," *family* + "-arches," *head, chief.*

   When we gathered for Thanksgiving dinner, our great-grandfather, the family patriarch, always sat at the head of the table.

3. **anarchy** (an'ər kē) society without rule or government; lawlessness; disorder; confusion; chaos. From Greek "an-," *not* + "arch(os)," *rule, ruler.*

The king's assassination led to anarchy throughout the country.

4. **hierarchy** (hī′ə rär′kē, hī′rär-) any system of persons or things ranked one above another; formerly, rule by church leaders, especially a high priest. From Greek "hieros," *sacred* + "arch(os)," *rule, ruler.*

The new office hierarchy ranks assistant vice presidents over directors.

5. **monarchy** (mon′ər kē) rule or government by a king, queen, emperor, or empress. From Greek "mon(o)-," *one* + "arch(os)," *rule, ruler.*

The French Revolution ended with the overthrow of the monarchy.

6. **oligarchy** (ol′i gär′kē) rule or government by a few persons. From Greek "oligos," *few* + "arch(os)," *rule, ruler.*

After the revolution, an oligarchy of army officers ruled the newly liberated country.

7. **archbishop** (ärch′bish′əp) a bishop of the highest rank; chief bishop.

The archbishop meets with the bishops from his area once a month to discuss their concerns.

8. **matriarch** (mā′trē ärk′) the female head of a family or tribe. From Greek "matri-," *mother* + "-arches," *head, chief.*

The younger members of the clan usually seek out Grandma Josie, the family matriarch, for advice.

9. **archetype** (är′ki tīp′) the original pattern or model after which a thing is made; prototype. From Greek "arch(e)-," *first, original* + "typos," *mold, type*.

Odysseus is the archetype for James Joyce's Leopold Bloom in his novel *Ulysses*.

10. **archaic** (är kā′ik) marked by the characteristics of an earlier period; antiquated. From Greek "arch(aios)," *old, early, first*.

With the advent of the pocket calculator, the slide rule has become archaic.

Test 1: Matching Synonyms

Select the best synonym for each of the italicized words. Circle your response.

1. the *archbishop* of Canterbury
   a. oldest bishop
   b. youngest bishop
   c. highest-ranking bishop
   d. recently appointed bishop

2. a strong *monarchy*
   a. government by a president
   b. government by a consortium
   c. government by the proletariat
   d. government by a king or queen

3. an *archaic* device
   a. old-fashioned
   b. complicated
   c. expensive
   d. useful

4. a wise *patriarch*
   a. old woman
   b. general
   c. revolutionary
   d. male family head

5. the literary and social *archetype*
   a. concern
   c. prototype
   b. exhibition
   d. major problem
6. a state of *anarchy*
   a. hopefulness
   c. strict order
   b. lawlessness
   d. female control
7. a brutal *archenemy*
   a. less powerful enemy
   c. strict enemy
   b. chief enemy
   d. Gabriel
8. the iron-handed *oligarchy*
   a. government by few
   c. democracy
   b. communist state
   d. unstable government
9. a highly respected *matriarch*
   a. confidant
   c. male leader
   b. duke
   d. female family head
10. the strict governmental *hierarchy*
    a. leadership
    c. system of ranking
    b. promotions
    d. discipline

Answers: 1. c   2. d   3. a   4. d   5. c
6. b   7. b   8. a   9. d   10. c

Test 2: True/False

In the space provided, write T if the synonym or definition of the numbered word is true or F if it is false.

		T or F
1. PATRIARCH	male family head	_____
2. ARCHETYPE	model	_____

		T or F
3. ARCHENEMY	chief enemy	_____
4. MONARCHY	royal government	_____
5. OLIGARCHY	chaos	_____
6. ARCHBISHOP	church deacon	_____
7. MATRIARCH	wife and mother	_____
8. ANARCHY	political lawlessness	_____
9. HIERARCHY	higher orders	_____
10. ARCHAIC	old-fashioned	_____

Answers: 1. T   2. T   3. T   4. T   5. F
6. F   7. F   8. T   9. F   10. T

LESSON 9 🕐

"TO LIFE!": *BIO*

In 1763, the Scottish writer James Boswell was first introduced to the acclaimed English poet, playwright, and dictionary-maker Samuel Johnson, setting the stage for the birth of modern biography. From 1772 until Johnson's death in 1784, the two men were closely associated, and Boswell devoted much of his time to compiling detailed records of Johnson's activities and conversations. Seven years after Johnson's death, Boswell published his masterpiece, the *Life of Samuel Johnson.* The word "biography," *a written account of another person's life,* comes from the Greek root "bio," meaning *life,* and "graphy," meaning *writing.* Besides *life,* "bio" can also mean *living, living thing,* or *biological.*

A number of other important words come from "bio." Here's a list of eight of them. Read through the definitions and practice the pronunciations, then go on to the quizzes.

1. **biodegradable** (bī′ō di grā′də bəl) capable of being decomposed by living organisms, as paper and kitchen scraps are, as opposed to metals, glass, and plastics, which do not decay.

   After a long campaign, the local residents persuaded the supermarkets to use biodegradable paper bags rather than nondegradable plastic.

2. **biofeedback** (bī′ō fēd′bak′) a method of learning to modify one's own bodily or physiological functions with the aid of a visual or auditory display of one's brain waves, blood pressure, or muscle tension.

   Desperate to quit smoking, she made an appointment to try biofeedback.

3. **bioengineering** (bī′ō en′jə nēr′ing) the application of engineering principles and techniques to problems in medicine and biology.

   In the last few decades, bioengineering has made important progress in the design of artificial limbs.

4. **biological clock** (bī′ə loj′i kəl klok′) an innate system in people, animals, and organisms that causes regular cycles of function or behavior.

   Recently the term "biological clock" has

been used in reference to women in their late thirties and early forties who are concerned about having children before they are no longer able to reproduce.

5. **bionic** (bī on′ik) utilizing electronic devices and mechanical parts to assist humans in performing tasks, as by supplementing or duplicating parts of the body. Formed from "bio-" + "(electr)onic."

The scientist used a bionic arm to examine the radioactive material.

6. **biopsy** (bī′op sē) the excision for diagnostic study of a piece of tissue from a living body. From "bio-" + Greek "opsis," *sight, view.*

The doctor took a biopsy from the patient's lung to determine the nature of the infection.

7. **biota** (bī ō′tə) the plant and animal life of a region or period. From Greek "biote," *life,* from the root "bio."

The biota from the cliffside proved more useful for conservation than the biologists had initially suspected.

8. **biohazard** (bī′ ō haz′ərd) a disease-causing agent or organism, especially one produced by biological research; the health risk caused by such an agent or organism.

Will new technology like gene splicing produce heretofore unknown biohazards to threaten the world's population?

Test 1: Definitions

Select the word that best fits the definition. Write your answer in the space provided.

_____ 1. the excision for diagnostic study of a piece of tissue from a living body.
a. biopsy   b. bioengineering
c. incision

_____ 2. utilizing electronic devices and mechanical parts to assist humans in performing tasks.
a. biota b. bioengineering c. bionic

_____ 3. capable of decaying and being absorbed by the environment.
a. biogenic   b. biodegradable
c. bionic

_____ 4. a method of learning to modify one's own bodily or physiological functions.
a. autobiography b. biofeedback
c. biota

_____ 5. the application of engineering principles and techniques to problems in medicine and biology.
a. bioengineering b. autobiography
c. biometry

_____ 6. an innate system in people, animals, and organisms that causes regular cycles of function.
a. biota b. bionic c. biological clock

_____ 7. the plant and animal life of a region.
   a. biota   b. autobiography
   c. biometry
_____ 8. an agent or organism that causes a health risk.
   a. biopsy   b. biohazard   c. biota

Answers: 1. a   2. c   3. b   4. b   5. a
6. c   7. a   8. b

Test 2: True/False

In the space provided, write T if the definition of the numbered word is true or F if it is false.

		T or F
1. BIOPSY	tissue sample	_____
2. BIOTA	plants and animals	_____
3. BIOLOGICAL CLOCK	perpetual clock	_____
4. BIOHAZARD	health risk	_____
5. BIODEGRADABLE	capable of decomposing	_____
6. BIONIC	superhero	_____
7. BIOFEEDBACK	culinary expertise	_____
8. BIOENGINEERING	railroad supervision	_____

Answers: 1. T   2. T   3. F   4. T   5. T
6. F   7. F   8. F

LESSON 10 🕐

"SPEAK!": *DICT, DIC*

The earliest known dictionaries were found in the library of the Assyrian king at Nineveh. These clay tablets, inscribed with cuneiform writing dating from the seventh century B.C., provide important clues to our understanding of Mesopotamian culture. The first English dictionary did not appear until 1440. Compiled by the Dominican monk Galfridus Grammaticus, the *Storehouse for Children or Clerics,* as the title translates, consists of Latin definitions of 10,000 English words. The word "dictionary" was first used in English in 1526, in reference to a Latin dictionary by Peter Berchorius. This was followed by a Latin-English dictionary published by Sir Thomas Elyot in 1538. All these early efforts confined themselves to uncommon words and phrases not generally known or understood, because the daily language was not supposed to require explanation.

Today we understand the word "dictionary" to mean *a book containing a selection of the words of a language, usually arranged alphabetically, giving information about their meanings, pronunciations, etymologies, etc.; a lexicon.* The word comes from the Latin root "dictio," taken from "dicere," meaning *to say, state, declare, speak.* This root has given us scores of important English words. Below are eight for you to examine. After you read through their pronunciations and definitions, complete the self-tests.

1. **malediction** (mal'i dik'shən) a curse or the utterance of a curse. From Latin "male-," *evil* + "dictio," *speech, word.*

   After the witch delivered her malediction, the princess fell into a swoon.

2. **abdication** (ab'di kā'shən) the renunciation or relinquishment of something such as a throne, right, power, or claim, especially when formal.

   Following the abdication of Edward VIII for the woman he loved, his brother George VI assumed the throne of England.

3. **benediction** (ben'i dik'shən) the invocation of a blessing. From Latin "bene-," *well, good* + "dictio," *speech, word.*

   The chaplain delivered a benediction at the end of the service.

4. **edict** (ē'dikt) a decree issued by a sovereign or other authority; an authoritative proclamation or command

   Herod's edict ordered the massacre of male infants throughout his realm.

5. **predicate** (pred'i kāt') to proclaim, declare, or affirm; base or found.

   Your acceptance into the training program is predicated upon a successful personal interview.

6. **jurisdiction** (jŏŏr'is dik'shən) the right, power, or authority to administer justice.

The mayor's jurisdiction extends only to the area of the village itself; outside its limits, the jurisdiction passes to the town board.

7. **dictum** (dik'təm) an authoritative pronouncement; saying or maxim.

The firm issued a dictum stating that smoking was forbidden on the premises.

8. **predictive** (pri dik'tiv) indicating the future or future conditions; predicting.

Although the day was clear and balmy, the brisk wind was predictive of the approaching cold snap.

Test 1: Matching Synonyms

Match each of the following numbered words with its closest synonym. Write your answer in the space provided.

1. PREDICTIVE	a. assert		_____
2. EDICT	b. maxim		_____
3. PREDICATE	c. indicating the future		_____
4. BENEDICTION	d. authority		_____
5. ABDICATION	e. decree		_____
6. MALEDICTION	f. imprecation, curse		_____
7. DICTUM	g. blessing		_____
8. JURISDICTION	h. renunciation		_____

Answers: 1. c   2. e   3. a   4. g   5. h
6. f   7. b   8. d

Test 2: True/False

In the space provided, write T if the definition of the numbered word is true or F if it is false.

		T or F
1. PREDICTIVE	indicative of the future	_____
2. PREDICATE	declare	_____
3. EDICT	decree	_____
4. JURISDICTION	authority	_____
5. DICTUM	blessing	_____
6. ABDICATION	assumption	_____
7. MALEDICTION	machismo	_____
8. BENEDICTION	opening services	_____

Answers: 1. T   2. T   3. T   4. T   5. F
6. F   7. F   8. F

LESSON 11 🕐

"LEAD ON, MACDUFF!": *DUC, DUCT*

Aqueducts, artificial channels built to transport water, were used in ancient Mesopotamia, but the ones used to supply water to ancient Rome are the most famous. Nine aqueducts were built in all; eventually they provided Rome with about thirty-eight million gallons of water daily. Parts of several are still in use, supplying water to fountains in Rome. The word "aqueduct" comes from the Latin "aqua," meaning *water*, and "ductus," meaning *a leading* or *drawing off*.

A great number of powerful words are derived from the "duc, duct" root. Here are nine such words. Read through the definitions and practice the pronunciations. Try to use each word in a sentence of your own. Finally, work through the two self-tests at the end of the lesson to help fix the words in your memory.

1. **induce** (in do͞os′, -dyo͞os′) to influence or persuade, as to some action.

    Try to induce her to stay at least a few hours longer.
2. **misconduct** (mis kon′dukt) improper conduct or behavior.

    Such repeated misconduct will result in a reprimand, if not an outright dismissal.
3. **abduct** (ab dukt′) to carry (a person) off or lead (a person) away illegally; kidnap.

    Jason's mother was so fearful that he might be abducted by a stranger that she refused even to let him walk to school alone.
4. **deduce** (di do͞os′, -dyo͞os′) to derive as a conclusion from something known or assumed.

    The detective was able to deduce from the facts gathered thus far that the murder took place in the early hours of the morning.
5. **viaduct** (vī′ə dukt′) a bridge for carrying a road or railroad over a valley, gorge, or the

like, consisting of a number of short spans; overpass.

The city government commissioned a firm of civil engineers to explore the possibility of building a viaduct over the river.

6. **reductive** (ri duk′tiv) pertaining to or producing a smaller size. From Latin "reduct-, reducere," *to lead back*.

The new electronic copier had reductive and enlargement capabilities.

7. **seduce** (si dōōs′, -dyōōs′) to lead astray, as from duty or rectitude.

He was seduced by the prospect of gain.

8. **traduce** (trə dōōs′, -dyōōs′) to speak maliciously and falsely of; slander. From Latin "traducere," *to transfer, lead across*.

To traduce someone's character can do permanent harm to his or her reputation.

9. **ductile** (duk′til) pliable or yielding.

The new plastic is very ductile and can be molded into many forms.

Test 1: Matching Synonyms

Match each of the numbered words with the closest synonym. Write your answer in the space provided.

1. SEDUCE	a. overpass	_____
2. VIADUCT	b. shrinking	_____
3. INDUCE	c. kidnap	_____
4. REDUCTIVE	d. bad behavior	_____
5. TRADUCE	e. infer	_____
6. ABDUCT	f. entice	_____
7. MISCONDUCT	g. pliable	_____
8. DEDUCE	h. defame	_____
9. DUCTILE	i. persuade	_____

Answers: 1. f   2. a   3. i   4. b   5. h
6. c   7. d   8. e   9. g

Test 2: True/False

In the space provided, write T if the definition of the numbered word is true or F if it is false.

		T or F
1. DEDUCE	infer	_____
2. DUCTILE	pliable	_____
3. SEDUCE	lead astray	_____
4. REDUCTIVE	magnifying	_____
5. TRADUCE	malign	_____
6. VIADUCT	overpass	_____
7. ABDUCT	restore	_____
8. MISCONDUCT	improper behavior	_____
9. INDUCE	persuade	_____

Answers: 1. T   2. T   3. T   4. F   5. T
6. T   7. F   8. T   9. T

LESSON 12 🕐

"JUST THE FACTS, MA'AM": FAC, FACT, FECT

We have formed a great many important and useful words from the Latin "facere," *to make* or *do.* A "facsimile," for example, derives from the Latin phrase "fac simile," meaning *to make similar,* and has come to mean *an exact copy.* Since facsimile copiers and transmitters have become very common, "facsimile" is now generally shortened and changed in spelling to "fax."

Many potent words are derived from the "fac, fact, fect" root. Eight such words follow. Learn them by completing this lesson; then try to use the root to help you figure out other "fac, fact" words you encounter.

1. **factious** (fak'shəs) given to or marked by discord; dissenting. From Latin "factio," *act of doing or of making connections;* group or clique, derived from "facere," *to do* or *make.*

   Factious groups threatened to break up the alliance.

2. **factotum** (fak tō'təm) a person employed to do all kinds of work, as a personal secretary or the chief servant of a household.

   Jeeves was the model of a gentleman's gentleman—the indispensable factotum of the frivolous Bertie Wooster.

3. **factitious** (fak tish′əs) made artificially; contrived.

 The report was merely a factitious account, not factual at all.

4. **facile** (fas′il) moving or acting with ease; fluent. From Latin "facilis," *easy to do*, derived from "facere," *to do*.

 With his facile mind, he often thought of startlingly original solutions to old problems.

5. **artifact** (är′tə fakt′) any object made by human skill or art. From the Latin phrase "arte factum," (*something*) *made with skill*.

 The archaeologists dug up many artifacts from the ancient Indian culture.

6. **facsimile** (fak sim′ə lē) an exact copy, as of a book, painting, or manuscript; a method of transmitting typed or printed material by means of radio or telegraph.

 If they could not obtain a facsimile of the document by noon, the deal would fall through.

7. **putrefaction** (py$\overline{oo}$′trə fak′shən) the decomposition of organic matter by bacteria and fungi. From Latin "putrere," *to rot* + "factio," *act of doing*.

 Once the putrefaction of the compost pile was complete, the gardener used the rotted material to enrich the soil.

8. **prefect** (prē′fekt) a person appointed to any of various positions of command, authority, or superintendence. From Latin "praefectus," formed from "prae," *ahead*,

surpassing + "fectus," *doing* (from "facere," to do).

The prefect was appointed to a term of three years.

Test 1: Definitions

Select the word that best fits the definition. Write your answer in the space provided.

_____ 1. the decomposition of organic matter by bacteria and fungi
a. chemical analysis   b. hypothermia
c. putrefaction

_____ 2. not natural; artificial
a. factious   b. facile   c. factitious

_____ 3. an exact copy, as of a book, painting, or manuscript
a. factoid   b. facsimile   c. putrefactio

_____ 4. given to dissension or strife
a. facile   b. factious   c. obsequious

_____ 5. an object made by humans
a. artifact   b. factotum   c. factious

_____ 6. a person employed to do all kinds of work
a. facile   b. factotum   c. faculty

_____ 7. moving or acting easily
a. putrefaction   b. prefect   c. facile

_____ 8. someone appointed to any of various positions of command, authority, or superintendence
a. prefect   b. facile   c. factotum

Answers: 1. c   2. c   3. b   4. b   5. a
6. b   7. c   8. a

Test 2: True/False

In the space provided, write T if the definition of the numbered word is true or F if it is false.

			T or F
1.	FACTITIOUS	contrived	_____
2.	FACTOTUM	carrier	_____
3.	PUTREFACTION	rotting	_____
4.	ARTIFACT	machinery	_____
5.	FACSIMILE	instant transmission	_____
6.	PREFECT	administrator	_____
7.	FACTIOUS	dissenting	_____
8.	FACILE	fluent	_____

Answers: 1. T   2. F   3. T   4. F   5. F
6. T   7. T   8. T

LESSON 13 🕒

"ALWAYS FAITHFUL": *FEDER, FID, FIDE*

"Semper fidelis" is Latin for *always faithful.* The phrase is the motto of the United States Marine Corps and the title of an 1888 march by John Philip Sousa. This phrase, as with a number of useful words, comes from the Latin root "fid, fide," meaning *trust, faith.*

Below are seven words derived from this root. Read through the meanings, practice the pronunciations, and complete the self-tests that follow to help fix the words in your memory.

1. **fidelity** (fi del'i tē) faithfulness; loyalty.
   Dogs are legendary for their fidelity to their masters.
2. **fiduciary** (fi dōō'shē er'ē, -dyōō'-) a person to whom property or power is entrusted for the benefit of another; trustee. From Latin "fiducia," *trust,* related to "fidere," *to trust.*
   The bank's fiduciary administers the children's trust funds.
3. **infidel** (in'fi dl, -del') a person who does not accept a particular religious faith. From Latin "in," *not* + "fidelis," *faithful* (from "fide," *faith*).
   The ayatollah condemned Salman Rushdie as an infidel.
4. **perfidious** (pər fid'ē əs) deliberately faithless; treacherous. From Latin "perfidia" ("per-," *through* + "fide," *faith*).
   The perfidious lover missed no opportunity to be unfaithful.
5. **confide** (kən fīd') to entrust one's secrets to another. From Latin "confidere" ("con-," *with* + "fidere," *to trust*).
   The two sisters confided in each other.
6. **bona fide** (bō'nə fīd', bon'ə) genuine; real; in good faith.

To their great astonishment, the offer of a free vacation was bona fide.

7. **affidavit** (af'i dā'vit) a written declaration upon oath made before an authorized official. From a Medieval Latin word meaning (*he*) *has declared on oath,* from Latin "affidare," *to pledge on faith.*

In the affidavit, they swore they had not been involved in the accident.

Test 1: Matching Synonyms

Match each of the following numbered words with its closest synonym. Write your answer in the space provided.

1. CONFIDE	a. faithfulness	_____
2. FIDELITY	b. heathen	_____
3. BONA FIDE	c. declaration	_____
4. INFIDEL	d. entrust	_____
5. AFFIDAVIT	e. trustee	_____
6. PERFIDIOUS	f. genuine	_____
7. FIDUCIARY	g. faithless	_____

Answers: 1. d   2. a   3. f   4. b   5. c
6. g   7. e

Test 2: Matching Synonyms

Select the best synonym for each numbered word. Write your answer in the space provided.

_____ 1. BONA FIDE
       a. unauthorized c. real
       b. deboned   d. well-trained

_____ 2. PERFIDIOUS
       a. irreligious   c. loyal
       b. content   d. treacherous

_____ 3. FIDELITY
       a. loyalty   c. great affection
       b. alliance   d. random motion

_____ 4. FIDUCIARY
       a. bank teller   c. insurance
       b. trustee   d. default

_____ 5. INFIDEL
       a. warrior   c. heathen
       b. intransigent d. outsider

_____ 6. AFFIDAVIT
       a. affright   c. loyalty
       b. declaration   d. betrothal

_____ 7. CONFIDE
       a. combine   c. entrust
       b. recline   d. convert

Answers: 1. c   2. d   3. a   4. b   5. c
6. b   7. c

LESSON 14 🕐

"FLOW GENTLY, SWEET AFTON": *FLU*

In 1991, the upper fifth of working Americans took home more money than the other four-fifths put together—the highest proportion of wealthy people since the end of World War II. One word to describe such wealthy people is "affluent," *prosperous*. The word comes from the Latin root "fluere," meaning *to flow*. As a river would flow freely, so the money of the affluent flows easily.

Seven of the most useful and important words formed from the "flu" root follow. Study the definitions and read through the pronunciations. Then do the self-tests.

1. **flume** (flōōm) a deep, narrow channel containing a mountain stream or torrent; an amusement-park ride through a water-filled chute or slide.

   The adults steadfastly refused to try the log flume ride, but the children enjoyed it thoroughly.

2. **confluence** (kon′flōō əns) a flowing together of two or more streams; their place of junction.

   The confluence of the rivers is marked by a strong current.

3. **fluent** (flōō′ənt) spoken or written effortlessly; easy; graceful; flowing.

   Jennifer was such a fluent speaker that she was in great demand as a lecturer.

4. **fluctuation** (fluk′chōō ā′shən) continual change from one course, condition, etc., to another.

   The fluctuation in temperature was astonishing, considering it was still only February.

5. **fluvial** (flo͞o′vē əl) of or pertaining to a river; produced by or found in a river.

   The contours of the riverbank were altered over the years by fluvial deposits.
6. **influx** (in′fluks′) a flowing in.

   The unexpected influx of refugees severely strained the community's resources.
7. **flux** (fluks) a flowing or flow; continuous change.

   His political views are in constant flux.

Test 1: True/False

In the space provided, write T if the definition of the numbered word is true or F if it is false.

			T or F
1.	FLUCTUATION	change	_____
2.	FLUVIAL	deep crevasse	_____
3.	FLUENT	flowing	_____
4.	FLUX	flow	_____
5.	INFLUX	egress	_____
6.	CONFLUENCE	diversion	_____
7.	FLUME	feather	_____

Answers: 1. T   2. F   3. T   4. T   5. F
6. F   7. F

Test 2: Matching Synonyms

Select the best definition for each numbered word. Write your answer in the space provided.

1. FLUX	a. gorge	_____
2. CONFLUENCE	b. flowing easily	_____
3. FLUME	c. continual shift	_____
4. FLUCTUATION	d. an inflow	_____
5. FLUENT	e. a flow	_____
6. INFLUX	f. riverine	_____
7. FLUVIAL	g. convergence	_____

Answers: 1. e   2. g   3. a   4. c   5. b
6. d   7. f

LESSON 15 🕐

"IN THE BEGINNING": *GEN*

Genesis, the first book of the Old Testament, tells of the beginning of the world. The English word "genesis" is taken from the Greek word for *origin* or *source*. From the root "gen," meaning *beget, bear, kind,* or *race,* a number of powerful vocabulary builders has evolved.

Here are ten "gen" words. Study the definitions and practice the pronunciations to help you learn the words. To accustom yourself to using these new terms in your daily speech and writing, work through the two self-tests at the end of the lesson.

1. **gene** (jēn) the unit of heredity in the chromosomes that controls the development of inherited traits. From Greek "-genes," *born, begotten.*

The gene for color blindness is linked to the Y chromosome.

2. **engender** (en jen′dər) to produce, cause, or give rise to.

   Hatred engenders violence.

3. **gentility** (jen til′i tē) good breeding or refinement.

   Her obvious gentility marked her as a member of polite society.

4. **gentry** (jen′trē) wellborn and well-bred people; in England, the class under the nobility.

   In former times, the gentry lived on large estates with grand houses, lush grounds, and many servants.

5. **genus** (jē′nəs) the major subdivision of a family or subfamily in the classification of plants and animals, usually consisting of more than one species.

   The biologist assigned the newly discovered plant to the appropriate genus.

6. **genial** (jēn′yəl, jē′nē əl) cordial; favorable for life, growth, or comfort.

   Under the genial conditions in the greenhouse, the plants grew and flourished.

7. **congenital** (kən jen′i tl) existing at or from one's birth.

   The child's congenital defect was easily corrected by surgery.

8. **eugenics** (yōō jen′iks) the science of improving the qualities of a breed or species,

especially the human race, by the careful selection of parents.

Through eugenics, scientists hope to engineer a superior race of human beings.

9. **genealogy** (jē′nē ol′ə jē) a record or account of the ancestry and descent of a person, family, group, etc.; the study of family ancestries.

Genealogy shows that Franklin Delano Roosevelt was a cousin of Winston Churchill.

10. **congenial** (kən jēn′yəl) agreeable or pleasant; suited or adapted in disposition; compatible.

The student enjoyed the congenial atmosphere of the library.

Test 1: Definitions

Select the word that best fits the definition. Write your answer in the space provided.

_____ 1. the major subdivision of a family or subfamily in the classification of plants and animals.
  a. gene   c. genial
  b. genus   d. gentry

_____ 2. suited or adapted in disposition; agreeable.
  a. genial   c. genealogy
  b. congenital d. congenial

_____ 3. wellborn and well-bred people.
- a. gene
- c. nobility
- b. gentry
- d. gentility

_____ 4. the science of improving the qualities of a breed or species.
- a. genetics
- c. genealogy
- b. gentry
- d. eugenics

_____ 5. the unit of heredity transmitted in the chromosome.
- a. ancestry
- c. gene
- b. DNA
- d. genus

_____ 6. cordial; favorable for life, growth, or comfort.
- a. genial
- c. eugenics
- b. gentry
- d. hospitality

_____ 7. to produce, cause, or give rise to.
- a. gentility
- c. genealogy
- b. engender
- d. genial

_____ 8. a record or account of the ancestry of a person, family, group, etc.
- a. gene
- c. glibness
- b. genealogy
- d. gentry

_____ 9. good breeding or refinement.
- a. reductive
- c. gentility
- b. genus
- d. eugenics

_____ 10. existing at or from one's birth.
- a. congenital
- c. congenial
- b. genus
- d. gene

Answers: 1. b   2. d   3. b   4. d   5. c
6. a   7. b   8. b   9. c   10. a

Test 2: True/False

In the space provided, write T if the definition of the numbered word is true or F if it is false.

			T or F
1.	GENTRY	peasants	_____
2.	CONGENITAL	incurable	_____
3.	GENIAL	debased	_____
4.	GENE	genetic material	_____
5.	EUGENICS	matricide	_____
6.	GENTILITY	viciousness	_____
7.	GENEALOGY	family history	_____
8.	CONGENIAL	pleasant	_____
9.	GENUS	subdivision	_____
10.	ENGENDER	cease	_____

Answers: 1. F   2. F   3. F   4. T   5. F
6. F   7. T   8. T   9. T   10. F

6. ROOT POWER II

LESSON 1 🕐

"THIS WAY TO THE EGRESS": *GRAD, GRES, GRESS*

P. T. Barnum was a nineteenth-century American showman whose greatest undertaking was the circus he called "The Greatest Show on Earth." The circus, which included a menagerie that exhibited Jumbo the elephant and a museum of freaks, was famous all over the country. After its merger in 1881 with James Anthony Bailey's circus, the enterprise gained international renown. When Barnum's customers took too long to leave his famous exhibits, he posted a sign: "This way to the egress." Following the arrow in eager anticipation of a new oddity, the visitors were ushered through the egress—the exit.

Knowing that the root "grad, gres, gress" means *step, degree,* or *walk* might have given these suckers a few more minutes to enjoy the exhibits, and it can certainly help you figure out a number of powerful words. Here are nine words that use this Latin root. Study the definitions, practice the pronunciations, and work through the two self-tests.

1. **digress** (di gres', dī-) to wander away from the main topic. From Latin "digressus, digredi," *to walk away* ("di-," *away, apart* + "gressus, gredi," *to walk, step*).

   The manager cautioned her salespeople that they would fare better if they did not digress from their prepared sales talks.

2. **transgress** (trans gres', tranz-) to break or violate a law, command, moral code, etc. From Latin "transgressus, transgredi," *to step across.*

   Those who transgress the laws of their ancestors often feel guilty.

3. **retrograde** (re' trə grād') moving backward; having backward motion.

   Most of the townspeople regarded the new ordinance as a prime example of retrograde legislation.

4. **regression** (ri gresh'ən) the act of going or fact of having gone back to an earlier place or state.

   The child's regression could be seen in his thumbsucking.

5. **degrade** (di grād') to reduce the dignity of (someone); deprive (someone) of office, rank, or title; lower (someone or something) in quality or character.

   He felt they were degrading him by making him wash the dishes.

6. **Congress** (kong'gris) the national legislative body of the United States, consisting of

the Senate and the House of Representatives; (*lower case*) encounter; meeting.

Congress held a special session to discuss the situation in the Middle East.

7. **gradation** (grā dā′shən) any process or change taking place through a series of stages, by degrees, or gradually. From Latin "gradatio," *series of steps,* derived from "gradus," *step, degree.*

He decided to change his hair color by gradation rather than all at once.

8. **gradient** (grā′dē ənt) the degree of inclination, or the rate of ascent or descent, in a highway, railroad, etc.

Although they liked the house very much, they were afraid that the driveway's steep gradient would make it hard to park a car there in the winter.

9. **progressive** (prə gres′iv) characterized by progress or reform; innovative; going forward; gradually increasing.

The progressive legislation wiped out years of social inequity.

Test 1: Matching Synonyms

Match each of the following numbered words with its closest synonym. Write your answer in the space provided.

1. CONGRESS	a. backward moving	_____
2. REGRESSION	b. depart from a subject	_____
3. GRADIENT	c. disobey	_____
4. PROGRESSIVE	d. meeting	_____
5. DIGRESS	e. stage, degree	_____
6. GRADATION	f. reversion	_____
7. RETROGRADE	g. humiliate	_____
8. DEGRADE	h. innovative	_____
9. TRANSGRESS	i. incline	_____

Answers: 1. d   2. f   3. i   4. h   5. b
6. e   7. a   8. g   9. c

Test 2: Defining Words

Define each of the following words.

1. gradient _____
2. Congress _____
3. progressive _____
4. regression _____
5. retrograde _____
6. degrade _____
7. digress _____
8. gradation _____
9. transgress _____

Suggested Answers: 1. the degree of inclination, or the rate of ascent or descent, in a highway, etc.

2. the national legislative body of the United States; a meeting or assembly 3. characterized by reform; increasing gradually 4. the act of going back to an earlier place or state 5. moving backward; having backward motion 6. to reduce (someone) to a lower rank; deprive of office, rank, or title; to lower in quality or character 7. to wander away from the main topic 8. any process or change taking place through a series of stages, by degrees, or gradually 9. to break or violate a law, command, moral code, etc.

LESSON 2 🕐

"SPLISH, SPLASH, I WAS TAKING A BATH": *HYDRO, HYDR*

According to mythology, the ancient Greeks were menaced by a monstrous nine-headed serpent with fatally poisonous breath. Killing it was no easy matter: When you lopped off one head, it grew two in its place, and the central head was immortal. Hercules, sent to destroy the serpent as the second of his twelve labors, was triumphant when he burned off the eight peripheral heads and buried the ninth under a huge rock. From its residence, the watery marsh, came the monster's name, "Hydra," from the Greek root "hydr(o)," meaning *water*.

Quite a few words are formed from the "hydro" or "hydr" root. Here are ten of them.

Read through the definitions, practice the pronunciations, and then work through the two self-tests that follow.

1. **hydrostat** (hī′drə stat′) an electrical device for detecting the presence of water, as from an overflow or a leak.

   The plumber used a hydrostat to locate the source of the leak in the bathroom.

2. **dehydrate** (dē hī′drāt) to deprive of water; dry out.

   Aside from being tasty and nutritious, dehydrated fruits and vegetables are easy to store and carry.

3. **hydrophobia** (hī′drə fō′bē ə) the disease rabies.

   Sufferers from hydrophobia are unable to swallow water.

4. **hydroplane** (hī′drə plān′) a light, high-powered boat, especially one with hydrofoils or a stepped bottom, designed to travel at very high speeds.

   The shore police acquired a new hydroplane to help them apprehend boaters who misuse the waterways.

5. **hydroponics** (hī′drə pon′iks) the cultivation of plants by placing the roots in liquid nutrients rather than soil.

   Some scientists predict that in the future, as arable land becomes increasingly more scarce, most of our vegetables will be grown through hydroponics.

6. **hydropower** (hī'drə pou'ər) electricity generated by falling water or another hydraulic source.

Hydropower is efficient, clean, and economical.

7. **hydrate** (hī'drāt) to combine with water.

Lime is hydrated for use in plaster, mortar, and cement.

8. **hydrangea** (hī drān'jə) a showy shrub cultivated for its large white, pink, or blue flower clusters. From Greek "hydr-," *water* + "angeion," *vessel*.

Hydrangeas require a great deal of water to flourish.

9. **hydrotherapy** (hī'drə ther'əpē) the treatment of disease by the scientific application of water both internally and externally.

To alleviate strained muscles, physical therapists often prescribe hydrotherapy.

10. **hydrosphere** (hī'drə sfēr') the water on or surrounding the surface of the planet Earth, including the water of the oceans and the water in the atmosphere.

Scientists are investigating whether the greenhouse effect is influencing the hydrosphere.

Test 1: Definitions

Select the word that best fits the definition. Write your answer in the space provided.

_____ 1. electricity generated by water
    a. hydropower   c. hydrotherapy
    b. hydrangea   d. electrolysis

_____ 2. the treatment of disease by the scientific application of water both internally and externally
    a. hydrate   c. hydrotherapy
    b. electrolysis d. hydroponics

_____ 3. a light, high-powered boat, especially one with hydrofoils or a stepped bottom
    a. hydropower c. hydroelectric
    b. hydroplane   d. hydroship

_____ 4. rabies; fear of water
    a. hydrate   c. hydroponics
    b. hydrother-
       apy   d. hydrophobia

_____ 5. the water on or surrounding the surface of the globe, including the water of the oceans and the water in the atmosphere
    a. hydrosphere c. hydrofoil
    b. hydrate   d. hydrangea

_____ 6. to deprive of water
    a. hydrate   c. hydrolyze
    b. dehydrate d. hydrotherapy

_____ 7. a showy shrub with large white, pink, or blue flower clusters
    a. hydrate   c. hydroponics
    b. hydrangea d. hydrofoil

_____ 8. the cultivation of plants by placing
the roots in liquid nutrient
solutions rather than soil
a. hydrother-   c. hydroponics
   apy
b. hydrangea   d. hydrolyze
_____ 9. to combine with water
a. hydrostat   c. hydrangea
b. hydrosphere d. hydrate
_____ 10. an electrical device for detecting
the presence of water, as from an
overflow or a leak
a. hydrosphere c. hydroponics
b. hydrangea   d. hydrostat

Answers: 1. a   2. c   3. b   4. d   5. a
6. b   7. b   8. c   9. d   10. d

Test 2: True/False

In the space provided, write T if the definition of
the numbered word is true or F if it is false.

		T or F
1. HYDROPOWER	hydroelectric power	_____
2. HYDROPLANE	boat	_____
3. HYDROPONICS	gardening in water	_____
4. HYDROSTAT	water power	_____
5. HYDRANGEA	flowering plant	_____
6. HYDROTHERAPY	water cure	_____
7. HYDRATE	lose water	_____
8. HYDROSPHERE	bubble	_____

		T or F
9. DEHYDRATE	wash thoroughly	_____
10. HYDROPHOBIA	pneumonia	_____

Answers: 1. T   2. T   3. T   4. F   5. T
6. T   7. F   8. F   9. F   10. F

LESSON 3 🕐

"AFTER ME, THE DELUGE": *LAV, LU*

The failure of Louis XV (1710–74) to provide strong leadership and badly needed reforms contributed to the crisis that brought about the French Revolution. Louis took only nominal interest in ruling his country and was frequently influenced by his mistresses. In the last years of his reign, he did cooperate with his chancellor to try to reform the government's unequal and inefficient system of taxation, but it was too late. His reported deathbed prophecy, "After me, the deluge," was fulfilled in the overthrow of the monarchy less than twenty years later. The word "deluge," meaning *flood,* comes from the Latin root "lu," *to wash.* As a flood, a deluge would indeed wash things clean.

A number of words were formed from the "lav, lu" root. Here are several examples. Study the definitions and practice the pronunciations. To help you remember the words, complete the two self-tests at the end of the lesson.

1. **dilute** (di lōōt′, dī-) to make thinner or weaker by adding water; to reduce the strength or effectiveness of (something). From Latin "dilutus, diluere," *to wash away*.

   The wine was too strong and had to be diluted.

2. **lavabo** (lə vä′bō, -vä′-) the ritual washing of the celebrant's hands after the offertory in the Mass; the passage recited with the ritual. From the Latin word meaning *I shall wash*, with which the passage begins.

   The priest intoned the Latin words of the lavabo.

3. **lavage** (lə väzh′) a washing, especially the cleansing of an organ, as the stomach, by irrigation.

   Lavage is a preferred method of preventing infection.

4. **diluvial** (di lōō′vē əl) pertaining to or caused by a flood or deluge.

   The diluvial aftermath was a bitter harvest of smashed gardens, stained siding, and missing yard furniture.

5. **alluvium** (ə lōō′vē əm) a deposit of sand, mud, etc., formed by flowing water.

   Geologists study alluvium for clues to the earth's history.

6. **ablution** (ə blōō′shən) a cleansing with water or other liquid, especially as a religious ritual; a washing of the hands, body, etc.

   He performed his morning ablutions with vigor.

Test 1: Matching Synonyms

Select the best or closest synonym for each numbered word. Write your answer in the space provided.

_____ 1. LAVAGE
       a. molten rock   c. washing
       b. sewage   d. religious ritual

_____ 2. ALLUVIUM
       a. great heat   c. flood
       b. rain   d. deposit of sand

_____ 3. LAVABO
       a. religious   c. flooding
          cleansing   d. lavatory
       b. volcano

_____ 4. ABLUTION
       a. cleansing   c. sacrifice
          with water   d. small font
       b. absence

_____ 5. DILUTE
       a. wash   c. cleanse
       b. weaken   d. liquefy

_____ 6. DILUVIAL
       a. before the   c. monarchy
          flood   d. of a flood
       b. antedate

Answers: 1. c   2. d   3. a   4. a   5. b
6. d

Test 2: True/False

In the space provided, write T if the definition of the numbered word is true or F if it is false.

			T or F
1.	DILUTE	reduce strength	_____
2.	DILUVIAL	two-lipped	_____
3.	LAVAGE	security	_____
4.	ALLUVIUM	molten rock	_____
5.	ABLUTION	washing	_____
6.	LAVABO	religious ritual	_____

Answers: 1. T   2. F   3. F   4. F   5. T
6. T

LESSON 4 🕐

"SILVER TONGUE": *LOQUI, LOQU, LOCU*

For many years, ventriloquist Edgar Bergen amused audiences as he tried to outwit his monocled wooden dummy, Charlie McCarthy. Among the most popular entertainers of his age, Bergen astonished audiences with his mastery of ventriloquism, the art of speaking so that projected sound seems to originate elsewhere, as from a hand-manipulated dummy. This ancient skill sounds easier than it is, since it requires modifying the voice through slow exhalation, minimizing movement of the tongue and lips, and maintaining an impassive expression to help shift viewers' attention to the illusory source of the voice.

The word "ventriloquism" comes from Latin "ventri-," *abdomen, stomach,* and the root "loqui," *to speak* (because it was believed that the ventriloquist produced sounds from his stomach). Many useful and important words were formed from the "loqui, loqu" root. Below are seven you should find especially helpful. Study the definitions and practice the pronunciations. To reinforce your learning, work through the two self-tests.

1. **obloquy** (ob′lə kwē) blame, censure, or abusive language.

    The vicious obloquy surprised even those who knew of the enmity between the political rivals.

2. **colloquial** (kə lō′kwē əl) characteristic of or appropriate to ordinary or familiar conversation rather than formal speech or writing.

    In standard American English, "He hasn't got any" is colloquial, while "He has none" is formal.

3. **soliloquy** (sə lil′ə kwē) the act of talking while or as if alone.

    A soliloquy is often used as a device in a drama to disclose a character's innermost thoughts.

4. **eloquent** (el′ə kwənt) having or exercising the power of fluent, forceful, and appropriate speech; movingly expressive.

William Jennings Bryan was an eloquent orator famous for his "Cross of Gold" speech.

5. **interlocution** (in'tər lō kyōō'shən) conversation; dialogue.

The interlocutions disclosed at the Watergate hearings riveted the American public to their TV sets.

6. **loquacious** (lō kwā'shəs) talking much or freely; talkative; wordy.

After the sherry, the dinner guests became loquacious.

7. **elocution** (el'ə kyōō'shən) a person's manner of speaking or reading aloud; the study and practice of public speaking.

After completing the course in public speaking, the pupils were skilled at elocution.

Test 1: Matching Synonyms

Match each of the numbered words with its closest synonym. Write your answer in the space provided.

1. LOQUACIOUS	a. censure	___
2. INTERLOCUTION	b. informal	___
3. ELOCUTION	c. monologue	___
4. COLLOQUIAL	d. talkative	___
5. SOLILOQUY	e. conversation	___
6. OBLOQUY	f. fluent	___
7. ELOQUENT	g. public speaking	___

Answers: 1. d 2. e 3. g 4. b 5. c
6. a 7. f

Test 2: Definitions

Select the word that best fits the definition. Write your answer in the space provided.

_____ 1. a person's manner of speaking or reading aloud; the study and practice of public speaking
   a. obloquy   c. prologue
   b. soliloquy   d. elocution

_____ 2. conversation; dialogue
   a. colloquial   c. monologue
   b. interlocution   d. elocution

_____ 3. tending to talk; garrulous
   a. eloquent   c. loquacious
   b. colloquial   d. elocutionary

_____ 4. characteristic of or appropriate to ordinary or familiar conversation rather than formal speech or writing
   a. colloquial   c. prologue
   b. eloquent   d. dialogue

_____ 5. the act of talking while or as if alone
   a. circumlocution   c. soliloquy
   b. dialogue   d. obloquy

_____ 6. having or exercising the power of fluent, forceful, and appropriate speech; movingly expressive
   a. interlocution   c. colloquial
   b. eloquent   d. loquacious

_____ 7. censure; abusive language
   a. interlocution   c. obloquy
   b. soliloquy   d. dialogue

LESSON 5 🕐

"STAR LIGHT, STAR BRIGHT": *LUC, LUX, LUM*

Before he was driven out of heaven because of his pride, Satan was called "Lucifer," which translates as *bringer of light.* In his epic retelling of the Bible, *Paradise Lost,* John Milton used the name "Lucifer" for the demon of sinful pride, and we call the planet Venus "Lucifer" when it appears as the morning star. "Lucifer" comes from the root "luc, lux" meaning *light.*

A number of powerful words derive from "luc" and its variations. We trust that you'll find the following seven *light* words "enlightening"! Study the definitions and practice the pronunciations. Then complete the two self-tests at the end of the lesson.

1. **pellucid** (pə lōō′ sid) allowing the maximum passage of light; clear.
    The pellucid waters of the Caribbean allowed us to see the tropical fish clearly.
2. **lucid** (lōō′sid) shining or bright; clearly understood.
    Stephen Hawking's lucid explanation of astrophysics became a bestseller.

3. **translucent** (trans lōō' sənt, tranz-) permitting light to pass through but diffusing it so that persons, objects, etc., on the opposite side are not clearly visible.

Frosted window glass is translucent.

4. **elucidate** (i lōō'si dāt') to make light or clear; explain.

Once my math teacher elucidated the mysteries of geometry, I had no further difficulty solving the problems.

5. **lucubrate** (lōō'kyōō brāt') to work, write, or study laboriously, especially at night. From Latin "lucubrare," *to work by artificial light*.

The scholar lucubrated for many long nights in an attempt to complete his thesis.

6. **luminary** (lōō'mə ner'ē) an eminent person; an object that gives light.

Certain that the elegant woman emerging from the limousine had to be a theatrical luminary, the crowd surged forward to get a closer look.

7. **luminous** (lōō'mə nəs) radiating or emitting light; brilliant.

The luminous paint emitted an eerie glow, not at all what the designer had envisioned.

Test 1: True/False

In the space provided, write T if the definition of the numbered word is true or F if it is false.

			T or F
1. LUCID	comprehensible		_____
2. ELUCIDATE	explain		_____
3. LUCUBRATE	lubricate		_____
4. PELLUCID	limpid, clear		_____
5. LUMINOUS	reflective		_____
6. LUMINARY	lightning		_____
7. TRANSLUCENT	opaque		_____

Answers: 1. T   2. T   3. F   4. T   5. F
6. F   7. F

Test 2: Matching Synonyms

Select the best definition for each numbered word. Write your answer in the space provided.

1. LUMINOUS	a. study hard	_____
2. ELUCIDATE	b. prominent person	_____
3. PELLUCID	c. brilliant	_____
4. LUCUBRATE	d. permitting but diffusing light	_____
5. LUCID	e. clearly understood	_____
6. LUMINARY	f. allowing the passage of maximum light	_____
7. TRANSLUCENT	g. clarify	_____

Answers: 1. c   2. g   3. f   4. a   5. e
6. b   7. d

LESSON 6 🕐

"EVIL BE TO HIM WHO DOES EVIL": *MALE, MAL*

"Malnutrition" is defined as *a lack of the proper type and amount of nutrients required for good health*. It is estimated that more than ten million American children suffer from malnutrition; the World Health Organization reports that over 600 million people suffer from malnutrition in the emerging countries alone. Malnourished people endure a variety of side effects, including a failure to grow, increased susceptibility to infection, anemia, diarrhea, and lethargy.

The root "mal" in the word "malnourished" means *bad, evil*, and words formed around this root invariably carry negative overtones. In Latin, the root is spelled "male"; in French, it's "mal," but regardless of the spelling, the root means *evil*. Study the definitions and pronunciations of the following "mal" words until you become comfortable with them. Then work through the two self-tests.

1. **maladjusted** (mal′ə jus′tid) badly adjusted.

   Despite attempts by the psychologist to ease him into his environment, the child remained maladjusted.

2. **malefactor** (mal′ə fak′tər) a person who violates the law; a criminal.

The police issued an all-points bulletin for the apprehension of the malefactor.

3. **maladroit** (mal′ə droit′) unskillful; awkward; clumsy.

With his large hands and thick fingers, the young man was maladroit at fine needlework.

4. **malevolent** (mə lev′ə lənt) wishing evil to another or others; showing ill will.

Her malevolent uncle robbed the heiress of her estate and made her a virtual prisoner.

5. **malapropism** (mal′ə prop iz′əm) a confused use of words, especially one in which one word is replaced by another of similar sound but ludicrously inappropriate meaning; an instance of such a use. The word comes from Mrs. Malaprop, a character in Sheridan's comedy *The Rivals* (1775), noted for her misapplication of words. Sheridan coined the character's name from the English word "malapropos," meaning *inappropriate*, derived from the French phrase "mal à propos," *badly (suited) to the purpose*.

"Lead the way and we'll precede" is a malapropism.

6. **malicious** (mə lish′əs) full of or characterized by evil intention.

The malicious gossip hurt the young couple's reputation.

7. **malfeasance** (mal fē′zəns) the performance by a public official of an act that is legally unjustified, harmful, or contrary to law.

Convicted of malfeasance, the mayor was sentenced to six months in jail.

8. **malignant** (mə lig'nənt) disposed to cause harm, suffering, or distress; tending to produce death, as a disease or tumor.

The patient was greatly relieved when the pathologist reported that the tumor was not malignant.

9. **malign** (mə līn') to speak harmful untruths about; slander.

"If you malign me again," the actor threatened the tabloid reporter, "I will not hesitate to sue."

Test 1: Matching Synonyms

Match each of the numbered words with its closest synonym. Write your answer in the space provided.

1. MALADROIT	a. wishing others evil	___
2. MALICIOUS	b. harmful; fatal	___
3. MALAPROPISM	c. official misconduct	___
4. MALFEASANCE	d. bungling, tactless	___
5. MALIGN	e. badly adjusted	___
6. MALIGNANT	f. spiteful	___
7. MALEFACTOR	g. criminal	___
8. MALEVOLENT	h. revile, defame	___
9. MALADJUSTED	i. confused use of words	___

Answers: 1. d   2. f   3. i   4. c   5. h
6. b   7. g   8. a   9. e

Test 2: True/False

In the space provided, write T if the definition of the numbered word is true or F if it is false.

		T or F
1. MALEFACTOR	ranger	_____
2. MALAPROPISM	faulty stage equipment	_____
3. MALFEASANCE	food poisoning	_____
4. MALICIOUS	spiteful	_____
5. MALADJUSTED	poorly adjusted	_____
6. MALIGNANT	benign	_____
7. MALADROIT	clumsy	_____
8. MALEVOLENT	bad winds	_____
9. MALIGN	defame	_____

Answers: 1. F   2. F   3. F   4. T   5. T
6. F   7. T   8. F   9. T

LESSON 7 🕐

"I DO!": *MATER, MATR*

The word "matrimony," meaning *marriage*, derives from the Latin root "mater," *mother*, because the union of a couple was established through motherhood. Most of us accept without question the idea of matrimony based on romantic love, but this is a relatively new belief. Only recently, following the rise of the middle class and the growth of democracy, has there been a tolerance of romantic marriages based on the free choice of the partners involved. Arranged marriages, accepted almost everywhere throughout history, eventually ceased to prevail in the West, although they persist in aristocratic circles to the present. The most extreme application of the custom of arranged marriages occurred in prerevolutionary China, where the bride and groom often met for the first time only on their wedding day.

We've inherited and created a number of significant words from the "mater, matr" root. Below are eight such words to help make your vocabulary more powerful and precise. Study the definitions and pronunciations; then complete the two self-tests.

1. **maternal** (mə tûr′nl) having the qualities of a mother; related through a mother.

    On his maternal side, he is related to Abigail and John Adams.

2. **matron** (mā′trən) a married woman, especially one with children, or one who has an established social position.

    The matrons got together every Thursday to play bridge or mahjong.

3. **mater** (mā′tər) informal or humorous British usage for "mother."

    "Mater is off to London again," said Giles, snidely.

4. **matrix** (mā′triks) that which gives origin or form to a thing, or which serves to enclose it.

Rome was the matrix of Western civilization.

5. **alma mater** (äl′mə mä′tər, al′-) a school, college, or university where a person has studied, and, usually, from which he or she has graduated. From the Latin phrase meaning *nourishing mother.*

Ellen's alma mater was Queens College.

6. **matrilineal** (ma′trə lin′ē əl, mā′-) inheriting or determining descent through the female line.

In a matrilineal culture, the children are usually part of the mother's family.

7. **matronymic** (ma′trə nim′ik) derived from the name of the mother or another female ancestor; named after one's mother. The word is also spelled "metronymic" (mē′trə nim′ik, me′-).

Some men have matronymic middle names.

8. **matriculate** (mə trik′yə lāt′) to enroll or cause to enroll as a student, especially in a college or university.

She intends to matriculate at City College in the fall.

Test 1: Definitions

Select the word that best fits the definition. Write your answer in the space provided.

_____ 1. that which gives origin or form to a thing, or which serves to enclose it
   a. matrix   c. mater
   b. matrimonial   d. alma mater

_____ 2. a school, college, or university at which a person has studied, and, usually, from which he or she has graduated
   a. maternal   c. maternity
   b. alma mater   d. matrimony

_____ 3. inheriting or determining descent through the female line
   a. femaleness   c. matrilineal
   b. matrix   d. lineage

_____ 4. derived from the name of the mother or another female ancestor; named after one's mother
   a. matriarch   c. alma mater
   b. matrilocal   d. matronymic

_____ 5. having the qualities of a mother
   a. alma mater   c. maternal
   b. matrilineal   d. matrix

_____ 6. a married woman, especially one with children, or one who has an established social position
   a. matrix   c. alma mater
   b. matron   d. homemaker

_____ 7. to enroll or cause to enroll as a student, especially in a college or university
   a. matriculate   c. matrix
   b. graduate   d. alma mater

_____ 8. informal British usage for "mother"
    a. mater   c. matron
    b. matriarch   d. ma

Answers: 1. a   2. b   3. c   4. d   5. c
6. b   7. a   8. a

Test 2: True/False

In the space provided, write T if the definition of the numbered word is true or F if it is false.

			T or F
1.	MATRIX	outer edges	_____
2.	ALMA MATER	stepmother	_____
3.	MATRILINEAL	grandmotherly	_____
4.	MATRICULATE	study for a degree	_____
5.	MATER	mother	_____
6.	MATERNAL	motherly	_____
7.	MATRONYMIC	from the mother's name	_____
8.	MATRON	single woman	_____

Answers: 1. F   2. F   3. F   4. T   5. T
6. T   7. T   8. F

LESSON 8 🕐

"BIRTH AND REBIRTH": *NASC, NAT*

The Renaissance (also spelled Renascence) occurred between 1300 and 1600, when the feudal society of the Middle Ages became an increasingly urban, commercial economy with a central political institution. The term "Renaissance," or *rebirth,* was first applied in the mid-nineteenth century by a French historian to what has been characterized as nothing less than the birth of modern humanity and consciousness. The word goes back to Latin "renasci," *to be reborn,* from "re-," *again* + "nasci," *to be born.*

Many significant words evolved from the "nasc, nat" root. Here are eight such words for your consideration. First, read through the pronunciations, definitions, and sentences. Then, to reinforce your reading, complete the two self-tests.

1. **natal** (nāt′l) of or pertaining to one's birth.
   The astrologer cast a natal chart for his client.
2. **nativity** (nə tiv′i tē, nā-) birth; the birth of Christ.
   The wanderer returned to the place of his nativity.
3. **nativism** (nā′ti viz′əm) the policy of protecting the interests of native inhabitants against those of immigrants.
   The supporters of nativism staged a protest to draw attention to their demands for protection against the newcomers.
4. **innate** (i nāt′) existing from birth; inborn.
   The art lessons brought out her innate talent.

5. **nascent** (nas′ənt, nā′sənt) beginning to exist or develop.

    The nascent republic petitioned for membership in the United Nations.

6. **nationalism** (nash′ə nl iz′əm, nash′nə liz′-) national spirit or aspirations; devotion to the interests of one's own nation. From Latin "natio," *nation, race,* derived from "nasci," *to be born.*

    Many Americans feel a stirring of nationalism when they see the flag or hear the national anthem.

7. **naturalize** (nach′ər ə līz′, nach′rə-) to invest (an alien) with the rights and privileges of a citizen. From Latin "natura," *birth, nature,* derived from "nasci," *to be born.*

    To become naturalized American citizens, immigrants have to study the Constitution of their adopted country.

8. **nee** (nā) born. The word is placed after the name of a married woman to introduce her maiden name. From French "née," going back to Latin "nata," *born,* from "nasci," *to be born.*

    Madame de Staël, nee Necker, was the central figure in a brilliant salon.

Test 1: True/False

In the space provided, write T if the definition of the numbered word is true or F if it is false.

			T or F
1. NATIVISM	protectionism		_____
2. NATURALIZE	admit to citizenship		_____
3. NEE	foreign wife		_____
4. NATAL	pertaining to birth		_____
5. NATIONALISM	immigration		_____
6. NATIVITY	rebirth		_____
7. NASCENT	native-born		_____
8. INNATE	inborn		_____

Answers: 1. T 2. T 3. F 4. T 5. F
6. F 7. F 8. T

Test 2: Matching Synonyms

Select the best definition for each numbered
word. Write your answer in the space provided.

1. INNATE	a. admit to citizenship	_____
2. NATIONALISM	b. relating to birth	_____
3. NATURALIZE	c. beginning to exist	_____
4. NEE	d. birth	_____
5. NATAL	e. protection of native inhabitants	_____
6. NASCENT	f. inborn	_____
7. NATIVISM	g. indicating maiden name	_____
8. NATIVITY	h. patriotism	_____

Answers: 1. f 2. h 3. a 4. g 5. b
6. c 7. e 8. d

LESSON 9 🕐

"DADDY DEAREST": *PATER, PATR*

To sociologists and anthropologists, patriarchy is a system of social organization in which descent is traced through the male line and all offspring have the father's name or belong to his people. Often, the system is connected to inheritance and social prerogatives, as in primogeniture, in which the eldest son is the sole heir. The ancient Greeks and Hebrews were a patriarchal society, as were the Europeans during the Middle Ages. While many aspects of patriarchy, such as the inheritance of the family name through the male line, persist in Western society, the exclusive male inheritance of property and other patriarchal customs are dying out.

From the "pater, patr" root, meaning *father*, we have formed many useful words. Eight of them follow. Go through the pronunciations, definitions, and sentences to help you make the words part of your daily speech and writing. Then complete the two self-tests.

1. **patrician** (pə trish'ən) a member of the original senatorial aristocracy in ancient Rome; any person of noble or high rank.

    You could tell she was a patrician from her elegant manner.

2. **expatriate** (*v.* eks pā'trē āt'; *n.* eks pā'trē it) to banish (a person) from his or her native

country; one who has left his or her native country.

Among the most famous American expatriates in the 1920s were the writers F. Scott Fitzgerald, Ernest Hemingway, and Gertrude Stein.

3. **patronage** (pā′trə nij, pa′-) the financial support or business afforded to a store, hotel, or the like, by customers, clients, or paying guests; the encouragement or support of an artist by a patron; the control of appointments to government jobs, especially on a basis other than merit alone. From Latin "patronus," *patron, protector, advocate,* derived from "pater," father.

To show its appreciation for its clients' patronage, the beauty shop offered a half-price haircut to all regular customers for the month of January.

4. **paternalism** (pə tûr′nl iz′əm) the system, principle, or practice of managing or governing individuals, businesses, nations, etc., in the manner of a father dealing benevolently and often intrusively with his children.

The employees chafed under their manager's paternalism.

5. **paternoster** (pā′tər nos′tər, pä′-, pat′ər-) the Lord's Prayer, especially in the Latin form. The term is often capitalized.

The term "paternoster" is a translation of the first two words of the prayer in the Vulgate version, "our Father."

6. **paterfamilias** (pā'tər fə mil'ē əs, pä'-, pat'ər-) the male head of a household or family.

   The paterfamilias gathered his children about him.

7. **patronymic** (pa'trə nim'ik) (a name) derived from the name of a father or ancestor, especially by the addition of a suffix or prefix indicating descent; family name or surname.

   Their patronymic was Williamson, meaning "son of William."

8. **patrimony** (pa'trə mō'nē) an estate inherited from one's father or ancestors; heritage.

   For his share of the patrimony, John inherited the family mansion at Newport.

Test 1: Definitions

Select the word that best fits the definition. Write your answer in the space provided.

_____ 1. the Lord's Prayer
     a. patrician   c. paternalism
     b. paternoster d. expatriate

_____ 2. derived from the name of a father or ancestor; family name or surname
     a. paterfamilias c. pater
     b. patronage   d. patronymic

_____ 3. the male head of a household or family
     a. paterfamilias c. patrician
     b. patronymic   d. patrimony

_____ 4. any person of noble or high rank
   a. patricide   c. expatriate
   b. patrician   d. patriot

_____ 5. the system, principle, or practice of managing or governing in the manner of a father dealing with his children
   a. paterfamilias c. paternalism
   b. expatriate   d. patronymic

_____ 6. to banish someone from his or her native country; one who has left his or her native country
   a. repatriate   c. paternalize
   b. patronize   d. expatriate

_____ 7. an estate inherited from one's father or ancestors; heritage
   a. patrimony   c. paternoster
   b. patricide   d. patronage

_____ 8. the financial support or business afforded to a store by its clients; the support of a patron; control of appointments to government jobs
   a. patronymic   c. patronage
   b. pater   d. paterfamilias

Answers: 1. b   2. d   3. a   4. b   5. c
6. d   7. a   8. c

Test 2: Matching Synonyms

Match each of the numbered words with its closest synonym. Write your answer in the space provided.

1. PATERNOSTER	a. financial backing	_____
2. PATRONYMIC	b. exile	_____
3. PATERFAMILIAS	c. male head of a family	_____
4. PATRIMONY	d. fatherly management	_____
5. PATRONAGE	e. the Lord's Prayer	_____
6. PATERNALISM	f. aristocrat	_____
7. PATRICIAN	g. surname	_____
8. EXPATRIATE	h. inheritance	_____

Answers: 1. e   2. g   3. c   4. h   5. a
6. d   7. f   8. b

LESSON 10 🕐

"KEEP ON TRUCKIN'": *PED, POD*

From the Latin root "ped" and the related Greek root "pod," both meaning *foot*, we have derived many words relating to movement by foot. The English word "foot" is itself a Germanic cousin of the Latin and Greek forms. One curious aberration is "peddler" (also spelled "pedlar," "pedler"), for it is *not* from the root "ped," as we would expect. The word may be derived from "pedde," a Middle English word for a lidless hamper or basket in which fish and other items were carried as they were sold in the streets, though it is generally thought to be of unknown origin.

The following eight words, however, all come from the "ped, pod" roots. Practice the pronunciations, study the definitions, and read the sentences. Then, to help set the words in your mind, complete the two self-tests that follow.

1. **quadruped** (kwod'rŏŏ ped') any animal, especially a mammal, having four feet.

   Horses, dogs, and cats are all classified as quadrupeds.

2. **podiatrist** (pə dī'ə trist) a person who treats foot disorders. From Greek "pod-," *foot* + "-iatros," *physician*.

   Podiatrists were formerly known as chiropodists.

3. **chiropodist** (ki rop'ə dist, kī-) a podiatrist. From Greek "cheir," *hand* + "podos," *foot*.

   A chiropodist treats minor problems of the feet, including corns and bunions.

4. **biped** (bī'ped) a two-footed animal.

   Humans are bipeds.

5. **expedient** (ik spē'dē ənt) tending to promote some desired object; fit or suitable under the circumstances. From Latin "expedire," *to make ready*, literally *to free the feet*.

   It was expedient for them to prepare all the envelopes at the same time.

6. **pseudopod** (sōō'də pod') an organ of propulsion on a protozoan.

   Amebas use pseudopods, literally "false feet," as a means of locomotion.

7. **pedigree** (ped'i grē') an ancestral line; lineage. From the French phrase "pied de

grue," *foot of a crane* (from the claw-shaped mark used in family trees to show lineage); "pied," *foot,* going back to the Latin root "ped."

The dog's pedigree could be traced six generations.

8. **pedometer** (pə dom′i tər) an instrument that measures distance covered in walking by recording the number of steps taken.

The race walker used a pedometer to keep track of how much distance she could cover in an hour.

Test 1: Definitions

Select the best definition for each numbered word. Write your answer in the space provided.

_____ 1. PEDIGREE
      a. dog training   c. horse racing
      b. lineage   d. nature walking

_____ 2. BIPED
      a. false feet   c. two-footed
      b. horses   animal
                      d. winged
                      creature

_____ 3. PEDOMETER
      a. race walking c. foot care
      b. jogger's   d. measuring
        injury   device

_____ 4. EXPEDIENT
      a. advantageous c. unnecessary
      b. extra careful d. walking swiftly

_____ 5. QUADRUPED
      a. four-footed   c. racehorse
         animal
      b. four-wheeled d. four animals
         vehicle

_____ 6. CHIROPODIST
      a. orthopedic   c. podiatrist
         surgeon   d. physician's
      b. chiropractor   assistant

_____ 7. PODIATRIST
      a. children's   c. chiropractor
         doctor
      b. foot doctor   d. skin doctor

_____ 8. PSEUDOPOD
      a. false seed   c. bad seed
         pod   d. organ of
      b. widow's peak   propulsion

Answers: 1. b   2. c   3. d   4. a   5. a
6. c   7. b   8. d

Test 2: True/False

In the space provided, write T if the definition of the numbered word is true or F if it is false.

		T or F
1. CHIROPODIST	foot doctor	_____
2. PEDIGREE	lineage	_____
3. EXPEDIENT	advantageous	_____
4. PODIATRIST	foot doctor	_____
5. QUADRUPED	four-footed animal	_____

			T or F
6.	PEDOMETER	scale	_____
7.	PSEUDOPOD	cocoon	_____
8.	BIPED	stereo	_____

Answers: 1. T   2. T   3. T   4. T   5. T
6. F   7. F   8. F

LESSON 11 🕐

"IT'S MY PLEASURE": *PLAC*

"S'il vous plaît," say the French to be polite. "Plaît" derives from "plaire," *to please,* which goes back to the Latin "placere." Thus the "plac" root, meaning *please,* forms the basis of the French expression for *if you please.* Many other words, including adjectives, nouns, and verbs, also derive from this root. Below are six "pleasing" words to add to your vocabulary. Look over the pronunciations, definitions, and sentences. Then to reinforce your study, complete the two self-tests.

1. **placid** (plas′id) pleasantly   peaceful   or calm.

   The placid lake shimmered in the early morning sun.
2. **complacent** (kəm plā′sənt) pleased, especially with oneself or one's merits, advantages, situation, etc., often without awareness of some potential danger, defect, or the like.

She stopped being so complacent after she lost her job.

3. **placebo** (plə sē′bō) a substance having no pharmacological effect but given to a patient or subject of an experiment who supposes it to be a medicine. From the Latin word meaning *I shall please.*

In the pharmaceutical company's latest study, one group was given the medicine; the other, a placebo.

4. **placate** (plā′kāt) to appease or pacify.

To placate an outraged citizenry, the Board of Education decided to schedule a special meeting.

5. **implacable** (im plak′ə bəl, -plā′kə-) incapable of being appeased or pacified; inexorable.

Despite concessions made by the allies, the dictator was implacable.

6. **complaisant** (kəm plā′sənt, -zənt, kom′plə zant′) inclined or disposed to please; obliging; gracious. From the French word for *pleasing,* derived ultimately from Latin "com- placere," *to be very pleasing.*

Jill's complaisant manner belied her reputation as a martinet.

Test 1: Synonyms

Select the best synonym for each numbered word. Write your answer in the space provided.

_____ 1. COMPLAISANT
    a. self-satisfied   c. agreeable
    b. fake   d. successful

_____ 2. IMPLACABLE
    a. obliging   c. calm
    b. foolish   d. inexorable

_____ 3. PLACID
    a. lake   c. wintery
    b. tranquil   d. nature-loving

_____ 4. COMPLACENT
    a. smug   c. contemplative
    b. wretched   d. obsessively neat

_____ 5. PLACEBO
    a. strong   c. sugar cube
      medicine   d. cure
    b. harmless
      drug

_____ 6. PLACATE
    a. offend   c. cause
    b. advertise   d. appease

Answers: 1. c   2. d   3. b   4. a   5. b
6. d

Test 2: Matching Synonyms

Match each of the numbered words with its closest synonym. Write your answer in the space provided.

1. PLACEBO   a. self-satisfied   _____
2. COMPLAISANT   b. serene   _____
3. IMPLACABLE   c. harmless substance _____

4. COMPLACENT	d. incapable of being appeased	_____
5. PLACATE	e. pacify	_____
6. PLACID	f. obliging	_____

Answers: 1. c   2. f   3. d   4. a   5. e
6. b

LESSON 12 🕐

"THE CITY OF BROTHERLY LOVE": *PHIL, PHILO*

The site of the future city of Philadelphia was settled in the mid-seventeenth century by Swedish immigrants. Later the prominent English Quaker William Penn (1644–1718) determined to establish a New World colony where religious and political freedom would be guaranteed. He first obtained from Charles II a charter for Pennsylvania (named by the king). In 1682 he surveyed the land and laid out the plan for the "City of Brotherly Love," Philadelphia. The settlement flourished from the time of its foundation, growing into a thriving center of trade and manufacturing.

The Greek root "phil, philo," meaning *love*, has given us many other words besides "Philadelphia." Here are ten of them to add to your vocabulary.

1. **philanthropy** (fi lan'thrə pē) affection for humankind, especially as manifested in

donations of money, property, or work to needy persons or for socially useful purposes. From Greek "philanthropia," *love of humanity*.

Millions of people have benefited from Andrew Carnegie's works of philanthropy.

2. **philanderer** (fi lan′dər ər) a man who makes love without serious intentions, especially one who carries on flirtations.

When she discovered that her husband was a philanderer, she sued for divorce.

3. **bibliophile** (bib′lē ə fīl′, -fil) a person who loves or collects books, especially as examples of fine or unusual printing, binding, or the like. From Greek "biblion," *book* + "philos," *loving*.

The bibliophile was excited by the prospect of acquiring a first edition of Mark Twain's *Life on the Mississippi*.

4. **philharmonic** (fil′här mon′ik) a symphony orchestra.

The philharmonic is presenting a concert this week.

5. **philately** (fi lat′l ē) the collection and study of postage stamps. From Greek "phil-," *loving* + "ateleia," *exemption from charges* (due to a sender's prepayment shown by a postage stamp).

To pursue his hobby of philately, the collector attended stamp exhibitions as often as possible.

6. **philhellene** (fĭl hel'ēn) a friend or supporter of the Greeks.

   George was a philhellene whose greatest
   passion was ancient Greek sculpture.

7. **philter** (fĭl'tər) a potion or drug that is
supposed to induce a person to fall in love
with someone.

8. **Anglophile** (ang'glə fīl', -fĭl) a person
who greatly admires England or anything
English.

   A devoted Anglophile, Barry visits England at least twice a year.

9. **philodendron** (fĭl'ə den'drən) an ornamental tropical plant.

   The word "philodendron" originally
   meant *fond of trees,* but now we use it to
   refer to a plant.

10. **philology** (fĭ lol'ə jē) the study of written
records, their authenticity and original form,
and the determination of their meaning; in
earlier use, linguistics. From Greek "philo-,"
loving + "logos," *word, speech, reason.*

Test 1: Definitions

Select the word that best fits the definition. Write
your answer in the space provided.

_____ 1. a person who greatly admires
England or anything English
a. Anglophile   c. bibliophile
b. philhellene   d. philanderer

_____ 2. an ornamental tropical plant
   a. philanthropy   c. philately
   b. philodendron   d. Anglophile
_____ 3. a love potion
   a. philhellene   c. philter
   b. philology   d. bibliophile
_____ 4. the collection and study of stamps
   a. philanthropy   c. philharmonic
   b. philology   d. philately
_____ 5. a symphony orchestra
   a. philodendron   c. philharmonic
   b. philter   d. philately
_____ 6. a friend and supporter of the Greeks
   a. philanderer   c. Anglophile
   b. philhellene   d. bibliophile
_____ 7. linguistics
   a. philter   c. philosophy
   b. philately   d. philology
_____ 8. a person who loves books
   a. philanderer   c. Anglophile
   b. philter   d. bibliophile
_____ 9. concern for humanity
   a. philanthropy   c. philology
   b. philodendron   d. philter
_____ 10. a man who makes love without serious intentions, especially one who carries on flirtations
   a. bibliographer   c. bibliophile
   b. philanderer   d. Anglophile

Test 1: True/False

In the space provided, write T if the definition of
the numbered word is true or F if it is false.

			T or F
1.	PHILATELY	fondness for stamps	_____
2.	PHILHELLENE	supporter of Greek culture	_____
3.	BIBLIOPHILE	lover of books	_____
4.	PHILANDERER	womanizer	_____
5.	PHILODENDRON	plant	_____
6.	PHILOLOGY	study of geography	_____
7.	PHILTER	filtration	_____
8.	PHILANTHROPY	stinginess	_____
9.	PHILHARMONIC	fond of books	_____
10.	ANGLOPHILE	stamp collector	_____

Answers: 1. T   2. T   3. T   4. T   5. T
6. F   7. F   8. F   9. F   10. F

LESSON 13 🕐

"HANG IN THERE, BABY!": *PEND*

The word "appendix" has two meanings. First, it
is an organ located in the lower right side of the
abdomen. A vestigial organ, it has no function in

humans. Second, it refers to the supplementary material found at the back of a book. The two meanings can be surmised from their root, "pend," *to hang* or *weigh*. The appendix (vermiform appendix, strictly speaking) "hangs" in the abdomen, as the appendix "hangs" at the end of a text.

Knowing the "pend" root can help you figure out the meanings of other words as well. Below are eight such words to help you hone your language skills.

1. **append** (ə pend′) to add as a supplement or accessory.

   My supervisor asked me to append this material to the report we completed yesterday.

2. **appendage** (ə pen′dij) a subordinate part attached to something; a person in a subordinate or dependent position.

   The little boy had been hanging on his mother's leg for so long that she felt he was a permanent appendage.

3. **compendium** (kəm pen′dē əm) a brief treatment or account of a subject, especially an extensive subject.

   The medical editors put together a compendium of modern medicine.

4. **stipend** (stī′pend) fixed or regular pay; any periodic payment, especially a scholarship allowance. From Latin "stips," *a coin* + "pendere," *to weigh, pay out.*

The graduate students found their stipends inadequate to cover the cost of living in a big city.

5. **pendulous** (pen'jə ləs, pend'yə-) hanging down loosely; swinging freely.

She had pendulous jowls.

6. **pendant** (pen' dənt) a hanging ornament.

She wore a gold necklace with a ruby pendant.

7. **impending** (im pen'ding) about to happen; imminent.

The impending storm filled them with dread.

8. **perpendicular** (pûr'pən dik'yə lər) vertical; upright.

They set the posts perpendicular to the ground.

Test 1: Matching Synonyms

Match each of the numbered words with its closest synonym. Write your answer in the space provided.

1. APPENDAGE	a. upright		_____
2. COMPENDIUM	b. salary		_____
3. IMPENDING	c. hanging		_____
4. PENDULOUS	d. adjunct		_____
5. PERPENDICULAR	e. ornament		_____
6. APPEND	f. summary		_____
7. PENDANT	g. attach		_____
8. STIPEND	h. imminently menacing		_____

Answers: 1. d   2. f   3. h   4. c   5. a
6. g   7. e   8. b

Test 2: True/False

In the space provided, write T if the definition of
the numbered word is true or F if it is false.

			T or F
1.	PENDULOUS	swinging freely	———
2.	PERPENDICULAR	curved	———
3.	PENDANT	hanging ornament	———
4.	STIPEND	fasten	———
5.	APPEND	add	———
6.	COMPENDIUM	excised section	———
7.	APPENDAGE	adjunct	———
8.	IMPENDING	imminent	———

Answers: 1. T   2. F   3. T   4. F   5. T
6. F   7. T   8. T

LESSON 14 🕐

"OH GOD!": *THE, THEO*

Atheism is the doctrine that denies the existence
of a supreme deity. Many people have been in-
correctly labeled atheists because they rejected
some popular belief in divinity. The Romans, for
example, felt the early Christians were atheists
because they did not worship the pagan gods;
Buddhists and Jains have been called atheistic

because they deny a personal God. The word "atheism" comes from the Greek prefix "a-," *without,* and the root "the, theo," meaning *god.*

Many words derive from this root; the following section provides just a few useful examples.

1. **theology** (thē ol'ə jē) the field of study that treats of the deity, its attributes, and its relation to the universe.
2. **theism** (thē'iz' əm) the belief in the existence of a God or deity as the creator and ruler of the universe.

    The religious seminary taught its students the philosophy of theism.
3. **monotheism** (mon'ə thē iz'əm) the doctrine or belief that there is only one God.

    Judaism and Christianity preach monotheism.
4. **theocracy** (thē ok'rə sē) a form of government in which God or a deity is recognized as the supreme ruler.

    Puritan New England was a theocracy, with ministers as governors and the Bible as the constitution.
5. **pantheism** (pan' thē iz'əm) the doctrine that God is the transcendent reality of which the material universe and human beings are only manifestations.

    The New England philosophy of Transcendentalism that flourished in the mid-nineteenth century included elements of pantheism.

6. **apotheosis** (ə poth′ē ō′sis, ap′ə thē′ə sis) the exaltation of a person to the rank of a god; ideal example; epitome.

   This poem is the apotheosis of the Romantic spirit.
7. **theogony** (thē og′ə nē) an account of the origin of the gods.

   Hesiod wrote a theogony of the Greek gods.

Test 1: Defining Words

Define each of the following words.

1. pantheism _____
2. theology _____
3. theogony _____
4. theism _____
5. apotheosis _____
6. theocracy _____
7. monotheism _____

Suggested Answers: 1. the doctrine that God is the transcendent reality of which the material universe and human beings are only manifestations 2. the field of study that treats of the deity, its attributes, and its relation to the universe 3. an account of the origin of the gods 4. the belief in one God as the creator and ruler of the universe 5. the exaltation of a person to the rank of a god; the glorification of a person, act, principle, etc., as an ideal 6. a form of government in which God or a deity is recognized as the supreme civil ruler 7. the doctrine or belief that there is only one God

Test 2: True/False

In the space provided, write T if the definition of the numbered word is true or F if it is false.

		T or F
1. APOTHEOSIS	epitome	_____
2. THEOGONY	account of the origin of the gods	_____
3. THEOCRACY	religious government	_____
4. THEISM	belief in rebirth	_____
5. MONOTHEISM	viral illness	_____
6. PANTHEISM	rejected beliefs	_____
7. THEOLOGY	study of divine things	_____

Answers: 1. T 2. T 3. F 4. F 5. F
6. F 7. T

LESSON 15 🕐

"CALL OUT!": *VOC*

The voice box (more properly called the "larynx") is the muscular and cartilaginous structure in which the vocal cords are located. The vibration of the vocal cords by air passing out of the lungs causes the formation of sounds that are then amplified by the resonating nature of the oral and nasal cavities. The root "voc," meaning *call* or *voice*, is the basis of words like "vocal," as well as a host of other powerful words. Now study the following ten "vocal" words.

1. **avocation** (av'ə kā'shən) a minor or occasional occupation; hobby. From Latin "avocatio," *distraction*, derived from "avocare," *to call away*.

   His avocation is bird-watching.

2. **vocable** (vō' kə bəl) a word, especially one considered without regard to meaning. From Latin "vocabulum," derived from "vocare," *to call*, from "voc-, vox," *voice*.

3. **vociferous** (vō sif'ər əs) crying out noisily; clamorous; characterized by noise or vehemence.

   She was vociferous in her support of reform legislation.

4. **advocate** (ad'və kāt') to plead in favor of; support.

   The citizens' committee advocated a return to the previous plan.

5. **convoke** (kən vōk') to summon to meet. From Latin "convocare" ("con-," *with, together* + "vocare," *to call*).

   They will convoke the members for a noon meeting.

6. **evoke** (i vōk') to call up, as memories or feelings. From Latin "evocare."

   The music evoked the mood of spring.

7. **revoke** (ri vōk′) to take back or withdraw; cancel. From Latin "revocare," *to call again, recall.*

   The king revoked his earlier decree.

8. **invoke** (in vōk′) to call forth or pray for; appeal to or petition; declare to be in effect. From Latin "invocare."

   The defendant invoked the Fifth Amendment so as not to incriminate himself.

9. **equivocal** (i kwiv′ə kəl) of uncertain significance; not determined; dubious. From Latin "aequivocus" ("aequus," *equal* + "voc-, vox," *voice*).

   Despite his demands for a clear-cut decision, she would give only an equivocal response.

10. **irrevocable** (i rev′ə kə bəl) incapable of being revoked or recalled; unable to be repealed or annulled.

    Once Caesar crossed the Rubicon, his decision to begin the civil war against Pompey was irrevocable.

Test 1: Matching Synonyms

Match each of the numbered words with its closest synonym. Write your answer in the space provided.

1. CONVOKE	a. word	_____
2. ADVOCATE	b. hobby	_____
3. REVOKE	c. uncertain	_____
4. EQUIVOCAL	d. permanent	_____
5. INVOKE	e. summon	_____
6. VOCABLE	f. pray for	_____
7. EVOKE	g. support	_____
8. VOCIFEROUS	h. loud	_____
9. IRREVOCABLE	i. cancel	_____
10. AVOCATION	j. call up; produce	_____

Answers: 1. e 2. g 3. i 4. c 5. f
6. a 7. j 8. h 9. d 10. b

Test 2: True/False

In the space provided, write T if the definition of the numbered word is true or F if it is false.

		T or F
1. REVOKE	restore	_____
2. AVOCATION	profession	_____
3. VOCIFEROUS	quiet	_____
4. ADVOCATE	oppose	_____
5. EVOKE	stifle	_____
6. EQUIVOCAL	unambiguous	_____
7. INVOKE	suppress	_____
8. IRREVOCABLE	changeable	_____
9. CONVOKE	summon	_____
10. VOCABLE	word	_____

LESSON 16 🕐

"A ROSE BY ANY OTHER NAME": *NOMIN, NOMEN*

The differences between the nominative and objective cases have baffled countless generations of English-speaking students. Is it I or me? Who or whom? The nominative case is so named because it *names* the subject, the doer of the action, whereas the objective case refers to the object, as of a verb or preposition. Here are eight words that use the root "nomin, nomen," *name.*

1. **nominee** (nom'ə nē') a person named, as to run for elective office or to fill a particular post.

    In order to qualify for consideration, the nominee was required to present a petition with three hundred verifiable signatures.
2. **misnomer** (mis nō'mər) a misapplied name or designation; an error in naming a person or thing.

    "Expert" was a misnomer; "genius" was a far more accurate description of the young chess player.
3. **nomenclature** (nō'mən klā'chər) a set or system of names or terms, as those used in a particular science or art.

The scientific nomenclature devised by Linnaeus was a great innovation.

4. **ignominious** (ig'nə min'ē əs) disgracing one's name; humiliating; discreditable; contemptible.

The army suffered an ignominious defeat.

5. **nominal** (nom'ə nl) being such in name only; so-called.

The silent partner is the nominal head of the firm.

6. **nominate** (nom'ə nāt') to name (someone) for appointment or election to office.

The delegate from Vermont was pleased to nominate a favorite son for President at the Democratic convention.

Test 1: True/False

In the space provided, write T if the definition of the numbered word is true or F if it is false.

		T or F
1. IGNOMINIOUS	foolish, ignorant	_____
2. NOMINATE	name as a candidate	_____
3. NOMENCLATURE	clamp	_____
4. NOMINEE	candidate	_____
5. NOMINAL	so-called	_____
6. MISNOMER	faux pas	_____

Answers: 1. F   2. T   3. F   4. T   5. T
6. F

Test 2: Synonyms

Select the best synonym for each numbered word. Write your answer in the space provided.

_____ 1. IGNOMINIOUS
  a. ignorant   c. disgraceful
  b. enormous   d. successful

_____ 2. NOMENCLATURE
  a. biology   c. torture device
  b. classification   d. international
                          transport

_____ 3. NOMINEE
  a. elected official c. candidate
  b. hereditary title d. assumed
                          name

_____ 4. MISNOMER
  a. misapplied name   c. wrong road
  b. married name   d. misapplied
                          remedy

_____ 5. NOMINAL
  a. a lot   c. so-called
  b. allot   d. summons

_____ 6. NOMINATE
  a. apply   c. reject
  b. designate   d. elect

Answers: 1. c   2. b   3. c   4. a   5. c
6. b

7. WORD HISTORIES I

LESSON 1 🕐

Words, like people, have a past, and as with people, some words have more interesting stories than others. Knowing a word's history can help you remember it and incorporate it into your daily speech. The following ten words have especially intriguing backgrounds. Read through the histories, then complete the self-tests that follow.

1. **bootlegger** (bōōt′leg′ər)
   Originally, a "bootlegger" was a person who smuggled outlawed alcoholic liquor in the tops of his tall boots. Today the term is used to mean *someone who unlawfully makes, sells, or transports alcoholic beverages* without registration or payment of taxes.

2. **bugbear** (bug′bâr′)
   The word refers to *a source of fears, often groundless*. It comes from a Welsh legend about a goblin in the shape of a bear that ate up naughty children.

3. **fiasco** (fē as′kō)
   "Fiasco" is the Italian word for *flask* or *bottle*. How it came to mean *a complete and ignominious failure* is obscure. One theory suggests that Venetian glassblowers set aside

fine glass with flaws to make into common bottles.

4. **jackanapes** (jak'ə nāps')

Today the word is used to describe *an impertinent, presumptuous young man; a whippersnapper*. Although its precise origin is uncertain, we know that the term was first used as an uncomplimentary nickname for William de la Pole, Duke of Suffolk, who was murdered in 1450. His badge was an ape's clog and chain. In a poem of the time, Suffolk was called "the Ape-clogge," and later referred to as an ape called "Jack Napes."

5. **jeroboam** (jer'ə bō'əm)

We now use the term "jeroboam" to refer to *a wine bottle having a capacity of about three liters*. Historically, Jeroboam was the first king of the Biblical kingdom of Israel, described in I Kings 11:28 as "a mighty man of valor," who, three verses later, "made Israel to sin." Some authorities trace the origin of today's usage to the king, reasoning that since an oversized bottle of wine can cause sin, it too is a jeroboam.

6. **nonplus** (non plus', non'plus)

The word "nonplus" means *to make utterly perplexed, to puzzle completely*. The original Latin phrase was "non plus ultra," meaning *no more beyond*, allegedly inscribed on the Pillars of Hercules, beyond which no ship could safely sail.

7. **quisling** (kwiz′ling)

This term refers to *a traitor,* a person who betrays his or her own country by aiding an enemy and often serving later in a puppet government. It is directly derived from the name of Vidkun Quisling (1887–1945), a Norwegian army officer turned fascist who collaborated with the Nazis early in World War II.

8. **bowdlerize** (bōd′lə rīz′, boud′-)

In 1818, Scottish physician Dr. Thomas Bowdler published a new edition of Shakespeare's works. The value of his edition, he stated, lay in the fact that he had edited it so that all "words and expressions are omitted which cannot with propriety be read aloud to the family." Good intentions aside, he found himself being held up to ridicule. From his name is derived the word "bowdlerize," meaning *to expurgate a literary text in a prudish manner.*

9. **boycott** (boi′kot)

In an attempt to break the stranglehold of Ireland's absentee landlords, Charles Stewart Parnell advocated in 1880 that anyone who took over land from which a tenant had been evicted for nonpayment of rent should be punished "by isolating him from his kind as if he was a leper of old." The most famous application of Parnell's words occurred soon after on the estate of the Earl of Erne. Unable to pay their rents, the earl's tenants suggested a lower scale, but the manager of the estate, Captain Charles Cunningham Boycott, would not accept the reduction. In retaliation, the tenants applied the measures proposed by Parnell, not only refusing to gather crops and run the estate, but also intercepting Boycott's mail and food, humiliating him in the street, and threatening his life. Their treatment of Boycott became so famous that within a few months the newspapers were using his name to identify any such nonviolent coercive practices. Today "boycott" means *to join together in abstaining from, or preventing dealings with, as a protest.*

10. **chauvinism** (shō'və niz'əm)
One of Napoleon's most dedicated soldiers, Nicolas Chauvin was wounded seventeen times fighting for his emperor. After he retired from the army, he spoke so incessantly of the majestic glory of his leader and the greatness of France that he became a laughingstock. In 1831, his name was used for a character in a play who was an almost idolatrous worshiper of Napoleon. The word "chauvin" became associated with this type of extreme hero worship and exaggerated patriotism. Today we use the term "chauvinism" to refer to *zealous and belligerent nationalism.*

Test 1: Matching Synonyms

Match each of the numbered words with its closest synonym. Write your answer in the space provided.

1. BOOTLEGGER	a. fanatical patriotism	___
2. BUGBEAR	b. total failure	___
3. FIASCO	c. expurgate	___
4. JACKANAPES	d. groundless fear	___
5. JEROBOAM	e. oversized wine bottle	___
6. NONPLUS	f. unlawful producer of alcohol	___
7. QUISLING	g. rude fellow	___
8. BOWDLERIZE	h. perplex	___
9. BOYCOTT	i. traitor	___
10. CHAUVINISM	j. strike	___

Answers: 1. f   2. d   3. b   4. g   5. e
6. h   7. i   8. c   9. j   10. a

Test 2: True/False

In the space provided, write T if the definition of the numbered word is true or F if it is false.

		T or F
1. BOWDLERIZE	expurgate	___
2. BOYCOTT	male child (Scottish)	___
3. BOOTLEGGER	petty thief	___
4. FIASCO	celebration	___

		T or F
5. CHAUVINISM	fanatical patriotism	_____
6. JACKANAPES	jack-of-all-trades	_____
7. QUISLING	turncoat	_____
8. BUGBEAR	baseless fear	_____
9. JEROBOAM	ancient queen	_____
10. NONPLUS	certain	_____

Answers: 1. T 2. F 3. F 4. F 5. T
6. F 7. T 8. T 9. F 10. F

LESSON 2 🕐

The origins of most of the following words can be
traced to Latin. Read through the histories, then
complete the self-tests.

1. **aberration** (ab'ə rā'shən)
   This word comes from the Latin verb "aber-
   rare," *to wander away from.* A person with a
   psychological "aberration" exhibits behavior
   that strays from the accepted path; hence the
   word means *deviation from what is common,
   normal, or right.*

2. **abominate** (ə bom'ə nāt')
   "Abominate" is from the Latin "abominor,"
   meaning *I pray that the event predicted by
   the omen may be averted.* The Romans mur-
   mured the word to keep away the evil spirits
   whenever anyone said something unlucky.
   Today we use it to mean *to regard with intense aversion or loathing; abhor.*

3. **abracadabra** (ab′rə kə dab′rə)

This intriguing-sounding word was first used as a charm in the second century. The Romans believed that the word had the ability to cure toothaches and other illnesses. Patients seeking relief wrote the letters in the form of a triangle on a piece of parchment and wore it around their necks on a length of thread. Today "abracadabra" is used as a pretend conjuring word. It also means *meaningless talk; nonsense.*

4. **wiseacre** (wīz′ā′kər)

Although the word "acre" in "wiseacre" makes it appear that the term refers to a unit of measurement, "wiseacre" is actually used contemptuously to mean *a wise guy* or *a smart aleck.* The term comes from the Dutch "wijssegger," which means *soothsayer.* Since soothsayers were considered learned, it was logical to call them "wise," which is what "wijs" means. The word "acre" is a mispronunciation of the Dutch "segger," *sayer.* There is a famous story in which the word was used in its present sense. In response to the bragging of a wealthy landowner, the English playwright Ben Jonson is said to have replied, "What care we for your dirt and clods? Where you have an acre of land, I have ten acres of wit." The chastened landowner is reported to have muttered: "He's Mr. Wiseacre."

5. **ebullient** (i bul′yənt, i bŏŏl′-)
   This word derives from the Latin "ebullire," *to boil over*. A person who is "ebullient" is *overflowing with fervor, enthusiasm, or excitement*.

6. **enclave** (en′klāv, än′-)
   The word "enclave" refers to *a country or territory entirely or mostly surrounded by another country*. More generally, it means *a group enclosed or isolated within a larger one*. The word comes ultimately from Latin "inclavare," *to lock in*.

7. **expedite** (ek′spi dīt′)
   The word "expedite" means *to speed up the progress of something*. It comes from the Latin "expedire," *to set the feet free*.

8. **expunge** (ik spunj′)
   To indicate that a soldier had retired from service, the ancient Romans wrote a series of dots or points beneath his name on the service lists. The Latin "expungere" thus meant both *to prick through* and *to mark off on a list*. Similarly, the English word "expunge" means *to strike or blot out; to erase*.

9. **inchoate** (in kō′it, -āt)
   "Inchoate" comes from the Latin "inchoare," *to begin*. Thus, an "inchoate" plan is *not yet fully developed*, or *rudimentary*.

10. **prevaricate** (pri var′i kāt′)
    Today "prevaricate" means *to speak falsely or misleadingly with deliberate intent; to lie*.

It has its origin in a physical act. The Latin verb "praevaricare" means *to spread apart*. The plowman who "prevaricated," then, made crooked ridges, deviating from straight furrows in the field.

Test 1: True/False

In the space provided, write T if the definition of the numbered word is true or F if it is false.

			T or F
1.	ENCLAVE	rendezvous	_____
2.	ABOMINATE	detest	_____
3.	WISEACRE	large ranch	_____
4.	EXPUNGE	erase	_____
5.	PREVARICATE	preplan	_____
6.	INCHOATE	illogical	_____
7.	ABERRATION	fidelity	_____
8.	EXPEDITE	slow down	_____
9.	ABRACADABRA	hocus-pocus	_____
10.	EBULLIENT	enthusiastic	_____

Answers: 1. F   2. T   3. F   4. T   5. F
6. F   7. F   8. F   9. T   10. T

Test 2: Matching Synonyms

Match each of the following numbered words with its closest synonym. Write your answer in the space provided.

1. WISEACRE	a. dispatch	_____
2. ENCLAVE	b. divergence	_____
3. INCHOATE	c. smarty-pants	_____
4. ABOMINATE	d. obliterate	_____
5. ABERRATION	e. misstate	_____
6. ABRACADABRA	f. enclosure	_____
7. EXPUNGE	g. detest	_____
8. EXPEDITE	h. mumbo-jumbo	_____
9. EBULLIENT	i. incipient	_____
10. PREVARICATE	j. high-spirited	_____

Answers: 1. c   2. f   3. i   4. g   5. b
6. h   7. d   8. a   9. j   10. e

LESSON 3 🕐

Powerful words may have their beginnings in historical events, myths and legends, and special terminology. Here are ten more powerful words with interesting or unusual histories. Read through the etymologies (word origins), then complete the self-tests that follow.

1. **impeccable** (im pek′ə bəl)
   The word comes from the Latin "impeccabilis," *without sin*. The religious meaning has been only slightly extended over the years. Today an "impeccable" reputation is *faultless, flawless, irreproachable*.

2. **ambrosia** (am brō′zhə)
   Originally, "ambrosia" was the food of the Olympian gods (as "nectar" was their drink).

The word comes from the Greek "a-," *not,* and "brostos," *mortal;* hence, eating ambrosia conferred immortality. Today the word means *an especially delicious food,* with the implication that the concoction is savory enough to be fit for the gods. One popular dessert by this name contains shredded coconut, sliced fruits, and cream.

3. **gerrymander** (jer'i man'dər, ger'-)
In 1812, Massachusetts governor Elbridge Gerry conspired with his party to change the boundaries of voting districts to enhance their own political clout. Noticing that one such district resembled a salamander, a newspaper editor coined the term "gerrymander" to describe *the practice of dividing a state, county, etc., into election districts so as to give one political party a majority while concentrating the voting strength of the other party into as few districts as possible.*

4. **mesmerize** (mez'mə rīz', mes'-)
The Austrian doctor Friedrich Anton Mesmer first publicly demonstrated the technique of hypnotism in 1775. Today the term "mesmerize" is still used as a synonym for "hypnotize," but it has broadened to also mean *spellbind* or *fascinate.*

5. **quintessence** (kwin tes'əns)
The word comes from the medieval Latin term "quinta essentia," *the fifth essence.* This fifth primary element was thought to be ether, supposedly the constituent matter of

the heavenly bodies, the other four elements being air, fire, earth, and water. The medieval alchemists tried to isolate ether through distillation. These experiments gave us the contemporary meaning of the word: *the pure and concentrated essence of a substance.*

6. **desultory** (des′əl tôr′ē)
Some Roman soldiers went into battle with two horses, so that when one steed wearied, the soldier could vault onto the second horse striding along parallel to the first without losing any time. The same skill was employed by circus performers, especially charioteers, who could leap between two chariots riding abreast. Such a skilled horseman was called a "desultor," *a leaper.* Perhaps because these equestrians stayed only briefly on their mounts, the word "desultory" acquired its present meaning, *lacking in consistency, constancy, or visible order.*

7. **aegis** (ē′jis)
When Zeus emerged victorious from his rebellion against the Titans, he attributed his success in part to his shield, which bore at its center the head of one of the Gorgons. The shield was reputedly made of goatskin, and hence its name, "aigis," was said to derive from the Greek "aig-," the stem of "aix," *goat.* Our present use of the word to mean *protection* or *sponsorship* evolved from the notion of 18th-century English writers who assumed that the "egis" of Zeus or Athena—

or their Roman counterparts Jove and Minerva—protected all those who came under its influence. Today the preferred spelling of the word is "aegis."

8. **adieu** (ə dōo′, ə dyōo′)
The French expression "à Dieu" literally means *to God.* It is an abbreviation of the sentence "Je vous recommande à Dieu," *I commend you to God,* used between friends at parting. Both in French and in English the word means *good-bye* or *farewell.*

9. **aloof** (ə lōof′)
The word was originally a sailor's term, "a loof," *to the luff or windward direction,* perhaps from the Dutch "te loef," *to windward.* Etymologists believe that our use of the word to mean *at a distance, especially in feeling or interest,* comes from the idea of keeping a ship's head to the wind, and thus clear of the lee shore toward which it might drift.

10. **bluestocking** (blōo′ stok′ing)
A "bluestocking" is *a woman with considerable scholarly, literary, or intellectual ability or interest.* The word originated in connection with intellectual gatherings held in London about 1750 in the homes of women bored by the more frivolous pastimes of their age. Lavish evening dress was not required at these affairs; in fact, to put at ease visitors who could not afford expensive clothing, the women themselves dressed

simply. One of the male guests went so far as to wear his everyday blue worsted stockings rather than the black silk ones usually worn at evening social gatherings. In response to their interests and dress, the English naval officer Admiral Edward Boscawen (1711–1761) is said to have sarcastically called these gatherings "the Blue Stocking Society."

Test 1: Definitions

Select the best definition for each numbered word. Circle your answer.

1. MESMERIZE
   a. attack
   b. burst forth
   c. fascinate
2. DESULTORY
   a. aggressive
   b. fitful
   c. nasty
3. ALOOF
   a. remote
   b. sailing
   c. windy
4. AEGIS
   a. intense interest
   b. goat
   c. sponsorship

5. GERRYMANDER
   a. medieval gargoyle
   b. combine for historical sense
   c. redistrict for political advantage
6. IMPECCABLE
   a. guileless
   b. perfect
   c. impeachable
7. ADIEU
   a. good-bye
   b. hello
   c. about-face
8. AMBROSIA
   a. suppository
   b. flower
   c. delicious food
9. QUINTESSENCE
   a. pith
   b. fruit
   c. oil
10. BLUESTOCKING
    a. ill-dressed woman
    b. intellectual woman
    c. poor man

Answers: 1. c   2. b   3. a   4. c   5. c
6. b   7. a   8. c   9. a   10. b

Test 2: Matching Synonyms

Select the best synonym for each numbered word. Write your answer in the space provided.

1. ADIEU	a. delicious food	_____
2. ALOOF	b. inconsistent; random	_____
3. GERRYMANDER	c. distant; remote	_____
4. AMBROSIA	d. farewell	_____
5. IMPECCABLE	e. sponsorship	_____
6. BLUESTOCKING	f. enthrall	_____
7. DESULTORY	g. without fault	_____
8. AEGIS	h. concentrated essence	_____
9. MESMERIZE	i. divide a political district	_____
10. QUINTESSENCE	j. a well-read woman	_____

Answers: 1. d   2. c   3. i   4. a   5. g
6. j   7. b   8. e   9. f   10. h

LESSON 4 ⏰

The following words are all based on Greek myths and legends. Read through their histories, then complete the self-tests.

1. **amazon** (am′ə zon′)
   The word comes ultimately from the Greek, but the origin of the Greek word is uncertain. "Amazon" refers to *a tall, powerful, aggressive woman*. The Amazons of legend were female warriors, allied with the Trojans against the Greeks.

2. **anemone** (ə nem′ə nē′)
   This spring flower is named for Anemone,

daughter of the wind. It comes from Greek "anemos," *the wind*.

3. **cornucopia** (kôr′nə kō′pē ə, -nyə-)
According to Greek mythology, to save the infant Zeus from being swallowed by his father, Cronus, his mother, Rhea, hid her son in a cave and tricked Cronus into swallowing a stone wrapped in a cloth. The infant was then entrusted to the care of the nymph Amaltheia, who fed him on goat's milk. One day she filled a goat's horn with fresh fruit and herbs. The horn was thereafter magically refilled, no matter how much the child ate. To the Greeks, this boundless source was the horn of Amaltheia; to the Romans, it was the "cornu copiae," from "cornu," *horn*, and "copia," *plenty*. We know a "cornucopia" as *a horn containing food or drink in endless supply* or *horn of plenty*. It is often used as a symbol of abundance.

4. **diadem** (dī′ə dem′)
In his quest to create a vast, unified empire with Babylon as its capital, the Macedonian hero Alexander the Great adopted a number of Persian and Oriental customs. He began to wear a blue-edged white headband with two ends trailing to the shoulders, a Persian symbol of royalty. The Greeks called this headpiece a "diadema," literally *a binding over*. The headpiece was adopted by other monarchs down through the ages and further embellished with gold and gems,

eventually evolving into a rich crown. Today a "diadem" is *a crown* or *a headband worn as a symbol of royalty.*

5. **epicure** (ep'i kyŏŏr')
Epicurus was a Greek philosopher who lived from 342 to 270 B.C. He believed that pleasure, attained mainly through pure and noble thoughts, constituted the highest happiness. After his death, his disciples spread his views. Their critics argued that Epicurus's theory was little more than an excuse for debauchery. From this argument we derive the present-day meaning of "epicure," *a person with luxurious tastes or habits, especially in eating or drinking.*

6. **esoteric** (es'ə ter'ik)
From the Greek "esoterikos," *inner*, the word was used to describe the secret doctrines taught by the philosopher Pythagoras to a select few of his disciples. Hence "esoteric" means *understood by or meant only for those who have special knowledge or interest; recondite.*

7. **labyrinth** (lab'ə rinth)
According to the Greek myth, King Minos of Crete ordered Daedalus to build a prison for the Minotaur, a half-bull, half-human monster. Daedalus succeeded by creating a series of twisting passageways that kept the monster imprisoned. Today a "labyrinth" is *a devious arrangement of linear patterns forming a design; a maze.*

8. **lethargy** (leth'ər jē)

The Greeks believed in an afterlife. In their mythology, the dead crossed the river Lethe, which flowed through Hades, the underground realm. Anyone who drank its water forgot the past. The Greek word "lethargia" derives from "lethe," *forgetfulness.* Hence our English word "lethargy," *drowsiness* or *sluggishness.*

9. **mentor** (men'tôr, -tər)

In the *Odyssey* of Homer, Mentor is Odysseus's friend and tutor to his son Telemachus. Today the word "mentor" means *trusted teacher or guide.*

10. **nemesis** (nem'ə sis)

Nemesis was the Greek goddess of vengeance, whose task it was to punish the proud and the insolent. Today a "nemesis" is *an agent or act of retribution or punishment,* or *something that a person cannot conquer or achieve.*

Test 1: True/False

In the space provided, write T if the definition of the numbered word is true or F if it is false.

			T or F
1.	DIADEM	crown	_____
2.	LABYRINTH	lazy	_____
3.	MENTOR	mendacious	_____
4.	AMAZON	female warrior	_____

		T or F
5. ANEMONE	mollusk	_____
6. ESOTERIC	arcane	_____
7. LETHARGY	lassitude	_____
8. NEMESIS	downfall	_____
9. CORNUCOPIA	foot ailment	_____
10. EPICURE	hidden	_____

Answers: 1. T   2. F   3. F   4. T   5. F
6. T   7. T   8. T   9. F   10. F

Test 2: Defining Words

Define each of the following words.

1. diadem _____
2. esoteric _____
3. mentor _____
4. nemesis _____
5. amazon _____
6. epicure _____
7. anemone _____
8. cornucopia _____
9. labyrinth _____
10. lethargy _____

Suggested Answers: 1. crown 2. meant only for the select few with special knowledge or interest 3. trusted teacher or guide 4. act of retribution, or that which a person cannot conquer or achieve 5. female warrior 6. a person with luxurious tastes or habits, especially in eating or drinking

7. flower   8. boundless source   9. maze 10. sluggishness; weariness

LESSON 5 🕐

Now study the curious origins of these ten words
and work through the two self-tests that follow.

1. **ostracize** (os'trə sīz')
   The word "ostracize" comes originally from
   the Greek "ostrakon," *tile, potsherd, shell.* It
   refers to the ancient Greek practice of ban-
   ishing a man by writing his name on a shell
   or a bit of earthen tile. Anyone considered
   dangerous to the state was sent into exile for
   ten years. The judges cast their votes by
   writing on the shells or pottery shards and
   dropping them into an urn. The word "ostracize" still retains the same sense, *to exclude,
   by general consent, from society.*

2. **sycophant** (sik'ə fənt, -fant')
   The word "sycophant" now means *a self-
   seeking, servile flatterer.* Originally, it was
   used to refer to an informer or slanderer.
   Curiously, it comes from Greek "sykon," *fig,*
   and "-phantes," *one who shows;* thus, *a fig-
   shower.* One explanation for this odd coin-
   age is that in ancient Greece a sycophant was
   an informer against merchants engaged in
   the unlawful exportation of figs.

3. **cynosure** (sī'nə shŏŏr', sin'ə-)
   According to the myth, Zeus chose to honor

the nymph who cared for him in his infancy
by placing her in the sky as a constellation.
One of her stars was so brilliant and station-
ary that all the other stars seemed to revolve
around it. To the practical-minded ancient
mariners, however, the bottom three stars
of the constellation looked like a dog's
tail. They named the entire constellation "Cynosura," *dog's tail*. From its name
we get our word "cynosure," *something
that attracts attention by its brilliance or
interest*. By the way, we now call the constellation "Ursa Minor," *Little Bear*, and
the bright star "Polaris," *Pole Star* or *North
Star*.

4. **belfry** (bel′frē)
Oddly enough, this word has nothing to do
with bells, except by association. Originally,
a "belfry" was a movable tower rolled up
close to the walls of a besieged city by soldiers in wartime. Later, a belfry was a tower
to protect watchmen, or a watchtower in
which alarm bells were hung, through which
usage it finally became *a bell tower*. The
word came into English from Old French,
which in turn may have taken it from a Germanic military term.

5. **debauch** (di bôch′)
Today we define the word "debauch" as *to
corrupt by sensuality, intemperance, etc.* It
comes from the French word "débaucher,"
meaning *to entice away from work or duty*.

6. **eldorado** (el′də rä′dō, -rä′-)

The word comes from Spanish legends of an incredibly wealthy city in South America, so rich that its streets were paved with gold. Many adventurers set off to find this elusive city; in 1595 Sir Walter Raleigh ventured into Guiana in a vain attempt to locate it. Among the Spaniards, the king of this fabulous land came to be called "El Dorado," *the Golden One*. Today "eldorado" is used generally to mean *any fabulously wealthy place*.

7. **esquire** (es′kwīər)

In medieval times, young men who wished to become knights first had to serve other knights. Their primary duty was to act as shield bearer. Because of this duty, the young man was called an "esquire," from the French "esquier," *shield bearer,* ultimately going back to the Latin "scutum," *shield*. Later the title "esquire" came to be attached to the sons of a nobleman; eventually it referred to any man considered a gentleman. Today it is often appended to a lawyer's name; in Britain, it is applied to a member of the gentry ranking next below a knight.

8. **filibuster** (fil′ə bus′tər)

In the seventeenth century, English seamen who attacked Spanish ships and brought back wealth from New Spain were called "buccaneers." In Holland, they were known as "vrijbuiters," *free robbers*. In French, the word became first "fribustier" and then "flibustier." In Spain, the term was "filibustero." Then, when the 19th-century American soldier of fortune William Walker tried to capture Sonora, Mexico, the Mexicans promptly dubbed him a "filibuster." Today the term refers to *the use of irregular or disruptive tactics, such as exceptionally long speeches, by a member of a legislative assembly.* The current use of the word may have arisen through a comparison of a legislator's determination to block a bill with the tactics used by William Walker to evade the law.

9. **furlong** (fûr′lông, -long)

In the twelfth century, an acre of land was defined as the area a yoke of oxen could plow in one day. As such, the size varied from place to place but always greatly exceeded what we accept today as an acre. In some places, an acre was defined by the area a team of eight oxen could plow in a day— about an eighth of a Roman mile, also called a "stadium." The length of the plow's furrows were thus each about a stadium in length; this became a convenient measure of distance—a "furlong" in Old English, from "furh," *furrow,* and "lang," *long.* This measure was then standardized to an area forty rods in length by four rods in width; however, the rod was not a standard measure either. Later, when the length of a yard was standardized, "furlong" came to be used simply as a term for *a unit of distance an eighth of a mile or 220 yards in length.*

10. **galvanism** (gal′və niz′əm)

In the mid-eighteenth century, Luigi Galvani, a professor of anatomy at the University of Bologna, concluded that the nerves are a source of electricity. Although Volta later proved his theory incorrect, Galvani's pioneering work inspired other scientists to produce electricity by chemical means. Today the term "galvanism," *electricity,* honors Galvani.

Test 1: Definitions

Each of the following phrases contains an italicized word. See how many you can define correctly. Write your answer in the space provided.

———— 1. bats in the *belfry*
    a. cave   c. bell tower
    b. brain   d. tropical tree

———— 2. *ostracized* from society
    a. banished   c. walked
    b. beaten   d. welcomed

———— 3. a hopeless *sycophant*
    a. dreamer   c. romantic
    b. alcoholic   d. toady

———— 4. travel a *furlong*
    a. acre   c. week
    b. year   d. less than a
                    mile

_____ 5. seek *eldorado*
    a. physical   c. wealthy place
       comfort   d. death
    b. delicious
       food

_____ 6. add the title *esquire*
    a. gentleman   c. duke
    b. married man   d. professional

_____ 7. *debauched* by the experience
    a. impoverished   c. strengthened
    b. corrupted   d. enriched

_____ 8. a lengthy *filibuster*
    a. entertainment   c. childhood
    b. obstructive   d. voyage
       tactics

_____ 9. powerful *galvanism*
    a. electric current   c. gases
    b. discoveries   d. weapons

_____ 10. the *cynosure* of all eyes
    a. defect   c. sky-blue color
    b. attraction   d. cynicism

Answers: 1. c   2. a   3. d   4. d   5. c
6. a   7. b   8. b   9. a   10. b

Test 2: True/False

In the space provided, write T if the definition of the numbered word is true or F if it is false.

		T or F
1. BELFRY	steeple	_____
2. DEBAUCH	corrupt	_____

		T or F
3. ESQUIRE	attorney's title	_____
4. OSTRACIZE	exclude	_____
5. FILIBUSTER	obstruction	_____
6. FURLONG	eighth of a mile	_____
7. CYNOSURE	sarcasm	_____
8. ELDORADO	Spain	_____
9. GALVANISM	atomic power	_____
10. SYCOPHANT	flatterer	_____

Answers: 1. T   2. T   3. T   4. T   5. T
6. T   7. F   8. F   9. F   10. T

LESSON 6 🕐

Our language is enriched by many exotic words with curious histories. Here are ten new ones to add to your growing vocabulary. Read through the etymologies and complete the two self-tests that follow.

1. **juggernaut** (jug'ər nôt', -not')
   Our modern word "juggernaut" comes from the Hindi name for a huge image of the god Vishnu, "Jagannath," at Puri, a city in Orissa, India. Each summer, the statue is moved to a new location a little less than a mile away from the old one. Early tourists to India brought back strange stories of worshipers throwing themselves under the wheels of the wagon carrying the idol. Since any shedding of blood in the presence of the god is sacri-

lege, what these travelers probably witnessed was a weary pilgrim being accidentally crushed to death. Thus, thanks to exaggeration and ignorance, "juggernaut" came to mean *blind and relentless self-sacrifice*. In addition, the word means *any large, overpowering, or destructive force*.

2. **iconoclast** (ī kon'ə klast')
An "iconoclast" is *a person who attacks cherished beliefs or traditional institutions*. It is from the Greek "eikon," *image*, and "klastes," *breaker*. Although the contemporary usage is figurative, the word was originally used in a literal sense to describe the great controversy within the Christian church in the eighth century over religious images. One camp held that all visual representations should be destroyed because they encouraged idol worship; the other, that such artworks simply inspired the viewers to feel more religious. By the mid-eighth century, untold numbers of relics and images had been destroyed. The issue was not settled for nearly a century, when the images were restored to the church in Constantinople.

3. **laconic** (lə kon'ik)
In Sparta, the capital of the ancient Greek region of Laconia, the children were trained in endurance, cunning, modesty, and self-restraint. From the terse style of speech and writing of the Laconians we derive the En-

glish word "laconic." Today the word retains this meaning, *expressing much in few words*.

4. **gamut** (gam'ət)
Guido of Arezzo, one of the greatest musicians of medieval times, is credited with being first to use the lines of the staff and the spaces between them. He used the Greek letter "gamma" for the lowest tone in the scale. This note was called "gamma ut." Contracted to "gamut," it then designated the entire scale. The word quickly took on a figurative as well as a literal sense. Today "gamut" is defined as *the entire scale or range*.

5. **guillotine** (gil'ə tēn', gē'ə-)
After the outbreak of the French Revolution, Dr. Joseph Ignace Guillotin became a member of the National Assembly. During an early debate, he proposed that future executions in France be conducted by a humane beheading machine that he had seen in operation in another country. His suggestion was received favorably; in 1791, after Dr. Guillotin had retired from public service, the machine that bears his name was designed by Antoine Louis and built by a German named Schmidt. The guillotine was first used in 1792 to behead a thief. At that time, the device was called a "Louisette" after its designer; but the public began calling it after Dr. Guillotin, the man who had first advocated its use.

6. **horde** (hôrd)

Upon the death of Genghis Khan, his grandson Batu Khan led the Mongol invasion of Europe, cutting a merciless swath from Moscow to Hungary. At each post, Batu erected a sumptuous tent made of silk and leather. His followers called it the "sira ordu," *the silken camp.* In Czech and Polish the Turkic "ordu" was changed to "horda." The name came to be applied not only to Batu's tent but also to his entire Mongol army. Because of the terror they inspired across the land, "horde" eventually referred to any Tartar tribe. Today, it means *any large crowd; swarm.*

7. **lyceum** (lī sē′əm)

The Lyceum was the shrine dedicated to Apollo by the Athenians. The name came from the Greek "Lykeion," meaning *Wolf Slayer,* a nickname of Apollo. The shrine was a favorite haunt of the Athenian philosophers, especially Aristotle, who taught his disciples while walking along its paths. Thus, the word "lyceum" came to mean *an institute for popular education, providing discussions, lectures, concerts, and so forth.*

8. **macabre** (mə kä′brə, -kä′bər)

In modern usage, "macabre" means *gruesome and horrible, pertaining to death.* Its history is uncertain. However, most etymologists believe that the word's use in the French phrase "Danse Macabré," *dance of Macabre,* a translation of Medieval Latin "chorea Macchabeorum," connects the word with the Maccabees, the leaders of the Jewish rebellion against Syria about 165 B.C., whose death as martyrs is vividly described in the Book of Maccabees (a part of the Apocrypha).

9. **gargantuan** (gär gan'chōō ən)

The sixteenth-century French writer François Rabelais created a giant he named "Gargantua" after a legendary giant of the Middle Ages. To fuel his enormous bulk— Gargantua rode on a horse as large as six elephants—he had to consume prodigious amounts of food and drink. Today we use the word "gargantuan" to mean *gigantic, enormous*.

10. **libertine** (lib'ər tēn')

In ancient Rome, "libertinus" referred to a freed slave. Since those freed from slavery were unlikely to be strict observers of the laws that had enslaved them in the first place, "libertine" came to designate *a person who is morally or sexually unrestrained*.

Test 1: Matching Synonyms

Match each of the numbered words with its closest synonym. Write your answer in the space provided.

1. LYCEUM	a. skeptic	_____
2. LIBERTINE	b. academy	_____
3. ICONOCLAST	c. overpowering force	_____
4. HORDE	d. terse	_____
5. GARGANTUAN	e. gruesome	_____
6. LACONIC	f. dissolute person	_____
7. GUILLOTINE	g. beheading machine	_____
8. JUGGERNAUT	h. entire range	_____
9. GAMUT	i. huge	_____
10. MACABRE	j. crowd	_____

Answers: 1. b   2. f   3. a   4. j   5. i
6. d   7. g   8. c   9. h   10. e

Test 2: Defining Words

Define each of the following words.

1. iconoclast _____
2. libertine _____
3. gamut _____
4. macabre _____
5. guillotine _____
6. laconic _____
7. gargantuan _____
8. lyceum _____
9. horde _____
10. juggernaut _____

Suggested Answers: 1. a person who attacks cherished beliefs or traditional institutions 2. a rake
3. the entire scale or range 4. horrible, gruesome

5. a machine used to behead criminals
6. terse 7. enormous, colossal 8. institute for popular education 9. large group 10. an overpowering force

LESSON 7 🕐

The English language has adopted a prodigious number of words from unexpected sources. Read through the histories of the ten unusual words that follow and then complete the self-tests.

1. **imp** (imp)
   In Old English, an imp was originally a young plant or seedling. Eventually, the term came to be used figuratively to indicate a descendant of a royal house, usually a male. Probably because of the behavior of such children, the word became synonymous with a young demon. Since the sixteenth century, the original meaning of "imp" as *scion* has been completely dropped, and the word is now used exclusively to mean *a little devil or demon, an evil spirit*, or *an urchin*.

2. **kaleidoscope** (kə lī′də skōp′)
   Invented in 1816 by Scottish physicist Sir David Brewster, the "kaleidoscope" is a scientific toy constructed of a series of mirrors within a tube. When the tube is turned by hand, symmetrical, ever-changing patterns can be viewed through the eyepiece. Brewster named his toy from the Greek "kalos,"

beautiful; "eidos," *form;* and "skopos," *watcher.*

3. **knave** (nāv)

In Old English, the word "knave" (then spelled "cnafa") referred to a male child, a boy. It was later applied to a boy or man employed as a servant. Many of these boys had to be wily to survive their hard lot; thus the word gradually evolved to mean *a rogue* or *rascal.*

4. **Machiavellian** (mak'ē ə vel'ē ən)

The Florentine political philosopher Niccolò Machiavelli (1469–1527) was a fervent supporter of a united Italy. Unfortunately, his methods for achieving his goals placed political expediency over morality. His masterpiece, *The Prince* (1513), advocated deception and hypocrisy on the grounds that the end justifies the means. Therefore, the adjective "Machiavellian" means *unscrupulous, cunning,* and *deceptive in the pursuit of power.*

5. **indolence** (in'dl əns)

Originally, "indolence" meant *indifference.* The word was used in that sense until the sixteenth century. Probably because indifference is frequently accompanied by an unwillingness to bestir oneself, the term has now come to mean *lazy* or *slothful.*

6. **incubus/succubus** (in'kyə bəs, ing'-; suk'yə bəs)

In the Middle Ages, women were thought to

give birth to witches after being visited in their sleep by an "incubus," or *evil male spirit*. The female version of this spirit, said to be the cause of nightmares, was a "succubus." Because the evil spirit pressed upon the sleeper's body and soul, the term "incubus" also means *something that oppresses like a nightmare*.

7. **hoyden** (hoid′n)

A "hoyden" is *a boisterous, ill-bred girl; a tomboy*. The word is usually linked to the Dutch "heyden," meaning *a rustic person or rude peasant*, originally *a heathen or pagan*, and is related to the English word "heathen." At first in English the word meant *a rude, boorish man*, but beginning in the 1600s it was applied to girls in the sense of *a tomboy*. How the change came about is uncertain.

8. **guinea** (gin′ē)

The guinea was a gold coin first minted in 1663 for the use of speculators trading with Africa. The coins were called "guineas" because the trade took place along the coast of Guinea. The British guinea came to be worth 21 shillings. After the establishment of the gold standard in the early nineteenth century, no more guineas were struck. In Great Britain, a pound and one shilling is still often called a "guinea."

9. **macadam** (mə kad′əm)

While experimenting with methods of improving road construction, John McAdam, a

Scotsman, concluded that the prevailing practice of placing a base of large stones under a layer of small stones was unnecessary. As surveyor-general for the roads of Bristol, England, in the early nineteenth century, McAdam built roads using only six to ten inches of small crushed stones, thereby eliminating the cost of constructing the base. Not only were the results impressive, the savings were so remarkable that his idea soon spread to other countries. McAdam's experiments led to our use of the term "macadam" for *a road surface* or *pavement*.

10. **mackintosh** (mak'in tosh')
In 1823, Scottish chemist Charles Macintosh discovered that the newfangled substance called "rubber" could be dissolved with naphtha. This solution could be painted on cloth to produce a waterproof covering. Clothing made from Macintosh's invention came to be called "mackintoshes," or *raincoats*.

Test 1: True/False

In the space provided, write T if the definition of the numbered word is true or F if it is false.

		T or F
1. INCUBUS	evil spirit	_____
2. HOYDEN	howl	_____

			T or F
3.	GUINEA	rush basket	_____
4.	MACADAM	raincoat	_____
5.	MACKINTOSH	road surface	_____
6.	IMP	male servant	_____
7.	MACHIAVELLIAN	principled	_____
8.	KALEIDOSCOPE	optical toy	_____
9.	INDOLENCE	laziness	_____
10.	KNAVE	dishonest fellow	_____

Answers: 1. T   2. F   3. F   4. F   5. F
6. F   7. F   8. T   9. T   10. T

Test 2: Matching Synonyms

Select the best definition for each numbered word. Write your answer in the space provided.

1.	MACADAM	a.	raincoat	_____
2.	HOYDEN	b.	little mischief-maker	_____
3.	GUINEA	c.	laziness	_____
4.	MACKINTOSH	d.	optical toy	_____
5.	MACHIAVELLIAN	e.	pavement	_____
6.	IMP	f.	rogue	_____
7.	KALEIDOSCOPE	g.	evil spirit	_____
8.	KNAVE	h.	gold coin	_____
9.	INDOLENCE	i.	sly and crafty	_____
10.	INCUBUS	j.	tomboy	_____

Answers: 1. e   2. j   3. h   4. a   5. i
6. b   7. d   8. f   9. c   10. g

LESSON 8 🕐

Now read about these ten words and complete the tests that follow.

1. **maelstrom** (māl′strəm)
   The word's figurative meaning, *a restless, disordered state of affairs*, is derived from its literal one. Today's meaning comes from "Maelstrom," the name of a strong tidal current off the coast of Norway. The current creates a powerful whirlpool because of its configuration. According to legend, the current was once so strong that it could sink any vessel that ventured near it.

2. **insolent** (in′sə lənt)
   The word comes from the Latin "insolentem," which literally meant *not according to custom*. Since those who violate custom are likely to offend, "insolent" evolved to imply that the person was also vain and conceited. From this meaning we derive our present usage, *contemptuously rude or impertinent in speech or behavior*.

3. **interloper** (in′tər lō′pər)
   The word "interloper" was used in the late sixteenth century to describe Spanish traders who carved out for themselves a piece of the successful trade the British had established with the Russians. The word was formed on the analogy of "landloper," meaning *one who trespasses on another's*

land, from a Dutch word literally meaning *land runner.* Although the dispute over the Spanish intrusion was settled within a few years, the word remained in use to mean *one who intrudes into some region or field of trade without a proper license* or *thrusts himself or herself into the affairs of others.*

4. **halcyon** (hal′sē ən)

According to classical mythology, the demigod Halcyone threw herself into the sea when she saw the drowned body of her beloved mortal husband. After her tragic death, the gods changed Halcyone and her husband into birds, which they called "halcyons," our present-day kingfishers. The Greeks believed the sea calmed as the birds built their nests and hatched their eggs upon its waves during the seven days before and after the winter solstice. This period came to be known as "halcyon days." The adjective is now used to mean *calm, peaceful, prosperous,* or *joyful.*

5. **hector** (hek′tər)

Hector was a great Trojan hero, son of King Priam. As Homer recounts in the *Iliad,* Hector took advantage of his enemy Achilles's departure from the Greek camp to drive the Greeks back to their ships and slay Achilles's dearest friend, Patroclus. To the Romans, who regarded themselves as descendants of the Trojans, Hector was a symbol of courage. But in the seventeenth century, the name was applied to the gangs of bullies who terrorized the back streets of London. It is to their transgressions that we owe the present use of "hector," *to harass or persecute.*

6. **helpmeet** (help′mēt′)
This synonym for *helpmate, companion, wife,* or *husband* is the result of a misunderstanding. The word comes from Genesis 2:18, "And the Lord God said, It is not good that the man should be alone; I will make him an help meet for him." In this passage, "meet" means *proper* or *appropriate,* but the two words came to be read as one, resulting in the word's current spelling.

7. **hermetic** (hûr met′ik)
The Greeks linked the Egyptian god Thoth with Hermes, calling him "Hermes Trismegistus," Hermes Three-Times Greatest. He was accepted as the author of the books that made up the sum of Egyptian learning, called the "Hermetic Books." Since these forty-two works largely concerned the occult sciences, "hermetic" came to mean *secret,* and in a later usage, *made airtight by fusion or sealing.*

8. **intransigent** (in tran′si jənt)
When Amadeus, the son of Victor Emmanuel II of Italy, was forced to abdicate the throne of Spain in 1873, those favoring a republic attempted to establish a political party. This group was called in Spanish "los intransigentes" (from "in-," *not* + "tran-

sigente," *compromising*) because they could not come to terms with the other political parties. The term passed into English as "intransigent." Today the word retains the same meaning: *uncompromising* or *inflexible.*

9. **jitney** (jit′nē)

The origin of this term has long baffled etymologists. The word first appeared in American usage in the first decade of the twentieth century as a slang term for a nickel. The word then became associated with the public motor vehicles whose fare was five cents. Some authorities have theorized that the term is a corruption of "jeton," the French word for *token.* Today a "jitney" is *a small passenger bus following a regular route at varying hours.*

10. **junket** (jung′kit)

At first, the word referred to a basket of woven reeds used for carrying fish, and was ultimately derived from Latin "juncus," *reed.* Then the basket was used to prepare cheese, which in turn came to be called "junket." Since the basket also suggested the food it could carry, "junket" later evolved to mean *a great feast.* Today we use the term in closely related meanings: *a sweet custardlike food* or *flavored milk curdled with rennet* or *a pleasure excursion.*

Test 1: Matching Synonyms

Match each numbered word with its closest synonym. Write your answer in the space provided.

1. HALCYON	a. tightly sealed	_____
2. INTRANSIGENT	b. intruder	_____
3. JITNEY	c. impertinent	_____
4. MAELSTROM	d. peaceful	_____
5. JUNKET	e. inflexible	_____
6. HECTOR	f. small bus	_____
7. INSOLENT	g. companion	_____
8. HERMETIC	h. pleasure trip	_____
9. INTERLOPER	i. harass	_____
10. HELPMEET	j. disorder	_____

Answers: 1. d   2. e   3. f   4. j   5. h
6. i   7. c   8. a   9. b   10. g

Test 2: True/False

In the space provided, write T if the definition of the numbered word is true or F if it is false.

		T or F
1. HALCYON	calm	_____
2. JITNEY	juggler	_____
3. MAELSTROM	masculine	_____
4. INTRANSIGENT	uncompromising	_____
5. INSOLENT	rude	_____
6. INTERLOPER	welcome guest	_____
7. JUNKET	refuse	_____

		T or F
8. HECTOR	helper	_____
9. HERMETIC	airtight	_____
10. HELPMEET	newcomer	_____

Answers: 1. T   2. F   3. F   4. T   5. T
6. F   7. F   8. F   9. T   10. F

LESSON 9 🕐

The interesting origins of these ten words can
help you remember their current meanings.
Complete the quizzes after your reading.

1. **knickers** (nik′ərz)
   The descendants of the Dutch settlers in
   New York are sometimes known as "Knicker-
   bockers." Thus, the term for the *loosely fit-
   ting short trousers gathered at the knee* that
   we call "knickers" derives from the name of
   the people who wore them, the Knicker-
   bockers. The pants first came to public attention in the illustrations to Washington
   Irving's *A History of New York from the Beginning of the World to the End of the Dutch
   Dynasty,* published in 1809 under the pen
   name Diedrich Knickerbocker. Knickers
   were formerly extremely popular attire for
   boys and young men.
2. **magenta** (mə jen′tə)
   On June 4, 1859, the French and Sardinian
   armies of Napoleon III won a decisive vic-

tory over the Austrian army in the northern fields of Italy near the small town of Magenta. At the time of the victory, scientists had just created a dye imparting a lovely reddish-purple color but had not yet named it. When the French chemists heard of the momentous triumph for their country, they named the dye "magenta" in honor of the victory. Today we call this *reddish-purple color* "magenta," but the dye itself is technically known as "fuchsin" (as in "fuchsia").

3. **garret** (gar'it)
   Originally, the French word "garite" referred to a watchtower from which a sentry could look out for approaching enemies. Among the things the Normans brought when they conquered England was the word "garite." In England the word came to mean a *loft* or *attic* and its spelling was altered to "garret."

4. **mandrake** (man'drāk)
   The original name for this narcotic herb was "mandragora," which is still its scientific name; the word comes from Greek "mandragoras," of unknown origin. In the Middle Ages, Englishmen erroneously assumed that "mandragora" came from "mandragon," a combination of "man," because of the appearance of its forked root, and "dragon," because of its noxious qualities. Since a dragon was then commonly called a "drake," the plant came to be called "mandrake."

5. **gazette** (gə zet′)

In the beginning of the sixteenth century, Venetians circulated a small tin coin of little value they called a "gazzetta," a diminutive of the word "gaza," magpie. Soon after, the government began to print official bulletins with news of battles, elections, and so forth. Because the cost of the newspaper was one gazzetta, the leaflet itself eventually came to be called a "gazzetta." By the end of the century, the term was used in England as well. The present spelling is the result of French influence. Today a "gazette" refers to *a newspaper* or *official government journal*.

6. **martinet** (mär′tn et′, mär′tn et′)

Seeking to improve his army, in 1660 Louis XIV hired Colonel Jean Martinet, a successful infantry leader, to devise a drill for France's soldiers. Martinet drilled his soldiers to such exacting standards that his name came to be applied to any officer intent on maintaining military discipline or precision. Thus, in English, a "martinet" is *a strict disciplinarian, especially a military one*. Interestingly, in France, Martinet's name acquired no such negative connotation.

7. **gorgon** (gôr′gən)

The name comes from the Greek myth of the three monstrous sisters who inhabited the region of Night. Together they were known as the "Gorgons"; their individual names were Stheno, Euryale, and Medusa. Little has been written about the first two. Medusa was the most hideous and dangerous; her appearance, with her head of writhing serpents, was so ghastly that anyone who looked directly at her was turned to stone. A secondary meaning of "gorgon" is *a mean or repulsive woman*.

8. **maudlin** (môd'lin)
This word, meaning *tearfully or weakly emotional*, comes from the miracle plays of the Middle Ages. Although these plays depicted many of the Biblical miracles, the most popular theme was the life of Mary Magdalene. The English pronounced her name "maudlin," and since most of the scenes in which she appeared were tearful, this pronunciation of her name became associated with mawkish sentimentality.

9. **meander** (mē an'dər)
In ancient times, the Menderes River in western Turkey was so remarkable for its twisting path that its Greek name, "Maiandros," came to mean *a winding*. In Latin this word was spelled "maeander," hence English "meander," used mainly as a verb and meaning *to proceed by a winding or indirect course*.

10. **gossamer** (gos'ə mər)
In fourth-century Germany, November was a time of feasting and merrymaking. The time-honored meal was roast goose. So many geese were eaten that the month came to be

called "Gänsemonat," *goose month*. The term traveled to England but in the course of migration, it became associated with the period of unseasonably warm autumn weather we now call "Indian summer." During the warm spell, large cobwebs are found draped in the grass or suspended in the air. These delicate, airy webs, which we call "gossamer," are generally believed to have taken their name from "goose summer," when their appearance was most noticeable. We now define "gossamer" as *something fine, filmy, or light;* it also means *thin and light*.

Test 1: Sentence Completion

Complete each sentence with the appropriate word from the following list.

gossamer	gorgon	knickers
magenta	maudlin	
mandrake	garret	meander
martinet	gazette	

1. It is pleasant to _____ slowly down picturesque country roads on crisp autumn afternoons.
2. The movie was so _____ that I was still crying when the closing credits began to roll.
3. The teacher was such a _____ that his students soon rebelled fiercely against his strict regulations.

4. In ancient days, the root of the _____ was surrounded by myths: it was believed that it could cast out demons from the sick, cause madness, or even make a person fall hopelessly in love.

5. Your entire load of white laundry will likely turn pink or even _____ if you include even a single new and previously unwashed red or purple sock.

6. Many budding artists have romantic fantasies about living in a wretched _____ and starving for the sake of their art.

7. Men rarely wear _____ any longer for playing golf, but the style was popular for many years.

8. The _____ cobwebs shredded at the slightest touch.

9. Since the daily _____ has excellent coverage of local sports, cultural events, and regional news, we tend to overlook its weak coverage of international events.

10. The gossip columnist was so mean and ugly that her victims referred to her as a

_____.

Answers: 1. meander 2. maudlin 3. martinet 4. mandrake 5. magenta 6. garret 7. knickers 8. gossamer 9. gazette 10. gorgon

Test 2: Definitions

Select the correct definition for each numbered word. Write your answer in the space provided.

_____ 1. KNICKERS
    a. short pants   c. early settlers
    b. soccer   d. punch line
       players

_____ 2. MEANDER
    a. moan   c. strike back
    b. ramble   d. starve

_____ 3. GORGON
    a. misunder-   c. hideous monster
       stood   d. midget
       person
    b. foregone
       conclusion

_____ 4. MAGENTA
    a. military   c. machinations
       victory   d. reddish-purple
    b. electricity   color

_____ 5. MANDRAKE
    a. myth   c. duck
    b. dragon   d. narcotic plant

_____ 6. GARRET
    a. basement   c. garage
    b. attic   d. unsuccessful
                  artist

_____ 7. MAUDLIN
    a. warlike   c. mawkish
    b. married   d. intense

_____ 8. MARTINET
    a. strict disci- c. hawk
       plinarian   d. musical
    b. facile   instrument
       problem

        a. journal   c. silver coin
        b. gazebo   d. book of maps
_____ 10. GOSSAMER
        a. variety of   c. flimsy material
           goose   d. idle talk
        b. grasp

Answers: 1. a   2. b   3. c   4. d   5. d
6. b   7. c   8. a   9. a   10. c

LESSON 10 🕐

Knowing the backgrounds of the following ten words will give you an edge in recalling their meanings and using them in conversation to make your speech and writing more powerful. When you have studied each word, complete the two quizzes that follow.

1. **meerschaum** (mēr'shəm, -shôm)
   Since it is white and soft and often found along seashores, ancient people believed this white claylike mineral was foam from the ocean turned into stone. As a result, in all languages it was called "sea foam." It was of little use until German artisans began to carve it into pipes, for as it absorbs the nicotine from the tobacco it acquires a deep honey color. Because the Germans were the first to find a use for it, the German name stuck: "meer," *sea;* "schaum," *foam.* In En-

glish "meerschaum" often means *a tobacco pipe with a bowl made of meerschaum* (the mineral).

2. **toady** (tō′dē)

In the seventeenth century, people believed that toads were poisonous, and anyone who mistakenly ate a toad's leg instead of a frog's leg would die. Rather than swearing off frogs' legs, people sought a cure for the fatal food poisoning. Charlatans would sometimes hire an accomplice who would pretend to eat a toad, at which point his employer would whip out his instant remedy and "save" his helper's life. For his duties, the helper came to be called a "toad-eater." Since anyone who would consume anything as disgusting as a toad must be completely under his master's thumb, "toad-eater" or "toady" became the term for *an obsequious sycophant; a fawning flatterer.*

3. **gregarious** (gri gâr′ē əs)

The Latin term for a herd of animals is "grex." Because a group of people banded together in military formation resembles a herd of animals, the word "grex" was applied to people as well as animals. The way the people grouped together was called "gregarius," *like a herd.* The word has come down to us as "gregarious," meaning *friendly* or *fond of the company of others.*

4. **miscreant** (mis′krē ənt)

The word's source, the Old French "mes-,"

wrongly, and "creant," *believing*, tells us that "miscreant" was originally used to describe a heretic. The word has evolved over the centuries, however, to refer to *a base, villainous, or depraved person.*

5. **sinecure** (sī'ni kyŏŏr', sin'i-)

"Sinecure," a word meaning *an office or position requiring little or no work, especially one yielding profitable returns*, originally began as a church term, from the Latin "beneficium sine cura," *a benefice without care*. It referred to the practice of rewarding a church rector by giving him a parish for which he had no actual responsibilities. The real work was carried on by a vicar, but his absent superior received the higher recompense. Although the church practice was abolished in the mid-nineteenth century, the term is often used today in a political context.

6. **ottoman** (ot'ə mən)

In the late thirteenth century, the Muslim Turks, under the leadership of Othman (also known as Osman I) established Turkey as "the Ottoman Empire." The empire was noted for its exotic silk and velvet furnishings. Travelers to the realm took some of their luxurious couches and divans back to Europe, where they became popular in France under the Bourbon kings. The French dubbed a *low, backless cushioned seat or footstool* an "ottomane" after its country of origin. The English called it an "ottoman."

7. **namby-pamby** (nam'bē pam'bē)

The term "namby-pamby," used to describe anything *weakly sentimental, pretentious, or affected,* comes from Henry Carey's parody of Ambrose Philips's sentimental children's poems. Carey titled his parody "Namby Pamby," taking the "namby" from the diminutive of "Ambrose" and using the first letter of his surname, "P," for the alliteration. Following a bitter quarrel with Philips, Alexander Pope seized upon Carey's parody in the second edition of his *Dunciad* in 1733. Through the popularity of Pope's poem, the term "namby-pamby" passed into general usage.

8. **mountebank** (moun'tə bangk')

During the Middle Ages, Italians conducted their banking in the streets, setting up business on convenient benches. In fact, the Italian word "banca" has given us our word "bank." People with less honest intentions realized that it would be relatively easy to cheat the people who assembled around these benches. To attract a crowd, these con men often worked with jugglers, clowns, rope dancers, or singers. Since they always worked around a bench, they were known as "montimbancos." Although the word was Anglicized to "mountebank," it still refers to *a huckster or charlatan* who sells quack medicines from a platform in a public place, appealing to his audience by using tricks, storytelling, and so forth.

9. **phaeton** (fā'i tn)

In Greek mythology, Helios drove the chariot of the sun across the sky each day. Helios's son Phaëton implored his father to let him drive the glittering chariot. Against his better judgment, one day Helios acceded to his son's wishes and let him drive the chariot pulled by its four powerful horses. Phaëton began well enough, but by midmorning he wearied and could no longer control the horses. The sun fluctuated between heaven and earth, causing great destruction. To stop the devastation, Zeus hurled a thunderbolt at Phaëton, who fell lifeless to the ground. In the sixteenth century, the English drew from this legend to describe a heedless driver as a "Phaeton." The word was later applied to *a light four-wheeled carriage* popular in the eighteenth century. Still later, it was applied to *a type of touring car.*

10. **mugwump** (mug'wump')

This word entered the English language in a most curious fashion. In the mid-1600s, the clergyman John Eliot, known as the Apostle to the Indians, translated the Bible into the Algonquian language. When he came to the thirty-sixth chapter of Genesis, he had no word for "duke," so he used "mugquomp," an Algonquian term for *chief* or *great man*. Historians of the language theorize that the term might already have been in circulation at that time, but they know for certain that by 1884 it was in fairly general use. In the presidential election that year, a group of Republicans threw their support to Grover Cleveland rather than to the party's nominee, James G. Blaine. The newspapers scorned the renegade Republicans as "mugwumps," those who thought themselves too good to vote for Blaine. The scorned Republicans got the last word when they adopted the same term to describe themselves, saying they were independent men proud to call themselves "mugwumps," or *great men*. Today we use the term "mugwump" to describe *a person who takes an independent position* or *one who is neutral on a controversial issue*.

Test 1: True/False

In the space provided, write T if the definition of the numbered word is true or F if it is false.

			T or F
1. TOADY	sycophant		_____
2. MISCREANT	sociable person		_____
3. MUGWUMP	political ally		_____
4. NAMBY-PAMBY	cereal		_____
5. GREGARIOUS	affable		_____

			T or F
6.	PHAETON	ghost	_____
7.	MOUNTEBANK	impostor	_____
8.	MEERSCHAUM	mixup	_____
9.	OTTOMAN	footstool	_____
10.	SINECURE	sincere	_____

Answers: 1. T   2. F   3. F   4. F   5. T
6. F   7. T   8. F   9. T   10. F

Test 2: Matching Synonyms

Match each of the following numbered words with its closest synonym. Write your answer in the space provided.

1.	MOUNTEBANK	a.	easy job	_____
2.	GREGARIOUS	b.	knave	_____
3.	OTTOMAN	c.	charlatan	_____
4.	TOADY	d.	carriage	_____
5.	MISCREANT	e.	sociable	_____
6.	MUGWUMP	f.	independent	_____
7.	NAMBY-PAMBY	g.	sycophant	_____
8.	SINECURE	h.	pipe	_____
9.	PHAETON	i.	low, backless seat	_____
10.	MEERSCHAUM	j.	sentimental	_____

Answers: 1. c   2. e   3. i   4. g   5. b
6. f   7. j   8. a   9. d   10. h

8. WORD HISTORIES II

LESSON 1 🕐

Here are ten new words to enhance your word power. When you have finished reading the history of each word, complete the self-tests.

1. **oscillate** (os′ə lāt′)
   In ancient Rome, the grape growers hung little images with the face of Bacchus, the god of wine, on their vines. Since the Latin word for face is "os," a little face would be called an "oscillum." Because the images swung in the wind, some students of language concluded that the Latin verb "oscillare" came from a description of this motion. Most scholars have declined to make this connection, saying only that our present word "oscillate," *to swing to and fro,* is derived from Latin "oscillare," *to swing,* which in turn comes from "oscillum," *a swing.*

2. **nabob** (nā′bob)
   The Mogul emperors, who ruled India from the sixteenth until the middle of the nineteenth century, delegated authority to men who acted as governors of various parts of India. To the native Indians, such a ruler was known as a "nawwab," *deputy.* The word was

changed by the Europeans into "nabob." The nabobs were supposed to tithe money to the central government, but some of the nabobs withheld the money, and thereby became enormously wealthy. From their fortunes came the European custom of using the word "nabob" to refer to a person, especially a European, who had attained great wealth in India or another country of the East. The usage spread to England, and today we use the term to describe *any very wealthy or powerful person*.

3. **pander** (pan′dər)

"Pander," *to act as a go-between in amorous intrigues* or *to act as a pimp or procurer* or *to cater basely*, comes from the medieval story of Troilus and Cressida. In his retelling, Chaucer describes how the love-stricken Troilus calls upon his friend Pandarus, kin to Cressida, to aid him in his quest for her love. Much of Chaucer's tale is devoted to the different means used by Pandarus to help Troilus win his love. Shakespeare later recycled the same legend. As the story gained in popularity the name "Pandarus" was changed in English to "pandare" and then to "pander." The noun now has the negative connotation of *pimp* or *procurer for illicit sexual intercourse*.

4. **pedagogue** (ped′ə gog′, -gôg′)

Wealthy Greek families kept a special slave to supervise their sons. The slave's responsibilities included accompanying the boys as they traveled to and from school and walked in the public streets. To describe a slave's chores, the Greeks coined the term "paidagogos," *a leader of boys.* Occasionally, when the slave was an educated man captured in warfare and sold into slavery, the slave also tutored his charges. From the Greek word we derived the English word "pedagogue," *teacher* or *educator.*

5. **quack** (kwak)

Noticing how the raucous shouts of the charlatans selling useless concoctions sounded like the strident quacks of ducks, the sixteenth-century Dutch called these charlatans "quacksalvers"—literally, *ducks quacking over their salves.* The term quickly spread through Europe. The English shortened it to "quack," and used it to describe *any fraudulent or ignorant pretender to medical skills,* the meaning we retain today.

6. **nepotism** (nep'ə tiz'əm)

This word for *patronage bestowed or favoritism shown on the basis of family relationships,* as in business or politics, can be traced to the popes of the fifteenth and sixteenth centuries. To increase their power, these men surrounded themselves with people they knew would be loyal—members of their own family. Among the most popular candidates were the popes' own illegitimate sons, called "nephews," from the Latin "nepos," *a descendant,* as a mark of respect. Eventually the term "nepotism" came to mean favoritism to all family members, not just nephews.

7. **pompadour** (pom'pə dôr', -dŏŏr')
Sheltered by a wealthy family and educated as though she were their own daughter, at twenty the exquisite Jeanne Antoinette Poisson Le Normant d'Étioles married her protector's nephew and began her reign over the world of Parisian fashion. Soon after, King Louis XV took her as his mistress, established her at the court of Versailles, and gave her the estate of Pompadour. The Marquise de Pompadour created a large and high-swept hairstyle memorialized by her name. Though it has been somewhat modified, the style is still known by her name.

8. **nostrum** (nos'trəm)
The word "nostrum," *a patent or quack medicine,* became very current around the time of the Great Plague in the mid-seventeenth century. Doctors were helpless to combat the disease, so charlatans and quacks scurried to fill the gap, flooding the market with their own "secret"—and useless—concoctions. To make their medicines seem more effective, they labeled them with the Latin word "nostrum." The term came to be used as a general word for any quack medicine.

Ironically, "nostrum" means *our own,* as in "nostrum remedium," *our own remedy;* thus it makes no claims at all for the remedy's effectiveness.

9. **narcissism** (när′sə siz′əm)

The word "narcissism," *inordinate fascination with oneself,* comes from the Greek myth of Narcissus. According to one version of the legend, an exceptionally handsome young man fell in love with his own image reflected in a pool. Because he was unable to embrace his image, he died from unrequited love. According to another version, Narcissus fell in love with his identical twin sister. After her death, he sat and stared at his own reflection in the pool until he died from grief.

10. **nepenthe** (ni pen′thē)

According to Greek legend, when Paris kidnapped Helen and took her to Troy, he wanted her to forget her previous life. In Homer's version of the tale, Paris gave Helen a drug thought to cause loss of memory. The drug was called "nepenthes." The word has come down to us with its meaning intact: *anything inducing a pleasurable sensation of forgetfulness.*

Test 1: True/False

In the space provided, write T if the definition of the numbered word is true or F if it is false.

		T or F
1. NEPENTHE	remembrance	_____
2. NEPOTISM	impartiality	_____
3. PANDER	procurer	_____
4. POMPADOUR	crewcut	_____
5. OSCILLATE	swing	_____
6. PEDAGOGUE	teacher	_____
7. NARCISSISM	self-love	_____
8. NABOB	pauper	_____
9. NOSTRUM	patent medicine	_____
10. QUACK	expert	_____

Answers: 1. F   2. F   3. T   4. F   5. T
6. T   7. T   8. F   9. T   10. F

Test 2: Defining Words

Define each of the following words.

1. pompadour _____
2. nepenthe _____
3. oscillate _____
4. nostrum _____
5. quack _____
6. nabob _____
7. pander _____
8. nepotism _____
9. pedagogue _____
10. narcissism _____

Suggested Answers: 1. upswept hairstyle 2. something inducing forgetfulness 3. to swing back and forth 4. patent or useless remedy 5. medical

charlatan 6. wealthy, powerful person 7. pimp or
procurer 8. patronage given to family members 9.
teacher 10. excessive self-love

LESSON 2 🕐

Each of these ten words beginning with the letter
"p" has a particularly captivating tale behind it.
Read the stories, then complete the two tests at
the end of the lesson.

1. **palaver** (pə lav′ər, -lä′vər)
   The word "palaver" derives ultimately from
   the Greek word "parabola," *comparison,* literally *a placing beside.* From this came English "parable," *a story that makes
   comparisons.* In Latin the word came to
   mean *speech, talk, word.* Later, Portuguese
   traders carried the term to Africa in the
   form "palavra" and used it to refer to the
   long talks with native chiefs required by local custom. English traders picked up the
   word in the eighteenth century, spelling it as
   we do today. The word retains its last meaning, *a long parley, especially one with people
   indigenous to a region* or *profuse, idle talk.*
2. **pannier** (pan′yər, -ē ər)
   The word "pannier" was first used in
   thirteenth-century France to mean *bread
   basket;* it is related to the French word
   "pain," *bread.* Soon it was also used to refer
   to a fish basket, and then a basket for toting

any provisions. In later centuries, the term was applied to the baskets balanced on a donkey's back. Today we use the term to denote *a basket, especially a large one carried on a person's back.*

3. **pariah** (pə rī′ə)
The term "pariah," *an outcast,* comes from the name of one of the lowest castes in India. Comprised of agricultural laborers and household servants, it is not the lowest caste, but its members are still considered untouchable by the Brahmans. The British used the term "pariah" for anyone of low social standing. The term "pariah" now is used for *any outcast among his or her own people.*

4. **pecuniary** (pi kyōo′nē er′ē)
The Romans measured a man's worth by the number of animals he kept on his farm. They adapted the Latin word for a farm animal, "pecu," to refer to individual wealth. But as people acquired new ways of measuring wealth, such as money and land, the Roman word evolved into "pecunia," which referred most specifically to money. From this came the adjective "pecuniary," *pertaining to or consisting of money.*

5. **phantasmagoria** (fan taz′mə gôr′ē ə)
In the early years of the nineteenth century, an inventor named Philipstal created a wondrous device for producing optical illusions. By projecting colored slides onto a thin silk

screen, Philipstal made his spectral images appear to move. Today, of course, we take such motion-picture illusions for granted, but in the age of the magic lantern, such visions were marvelous indeed. Philipstal named his invention "phantasmagoria," which we now apply to *a shifting series of phantasms or deceptive appearances, as in a dream.*

6. **poplin** (pop'lin)

The origin of this word has nothing to do with its appearance or use. In the early fourteenth century, the papal seat was located in Avignon, France. Even after the papacy was moved to Rome, Avignon remained important for its production of a sturdy dress and upholstery fabric. The fabric came to be identified with the city in which it was made. Since Avignon remained a papal town until the late eighteenth century, the fabric came to be called "papelino," or *papal*. The English pronounced the word "poplin," giving us the present-day name for this *finely corded fabric of cotton, rayon, silk, or wool.*

7. **precipitate** (pri sip'i tāt')

The word "precipitate" is based on the Latin root "caput," meaning *head*. In fact, the word was first used to apply to those who had been executed or killed themselves by being hurled or jumping headlong from a "precipice" or high place. Later, the word came to mean *to rush headlong*. From this has come today's meaning, *to hasten the occurrence of; to bring about prematurely.*

8. **precocious** (pri kō′shəs)

To the Romans, Latin "praecox," the source of English "precocious," was a culinary term meaning *precooked*. In time, however, its meaning was extended to *acting prematurely.* It is this later meaning of "precocious" that we use today, *unusually advanced in development, especially mental development.*

9. **pretext** (prē′tekst)

"Pretext" comes from the Latin word "praetexta," meaning *an ornament*, such as the purple markings on a toga denoting rank. In addition to its literal sense, however, the word carried the connotation of something to cloak one's true identity. We have retained only the word's figurative meaning, *something that is put forward to conceal a true purpose or object; an ostensible reason.*

10. **procrustean** (prō krus′tē ən)

According to one version of the Greek myth, Procrustes was a bandit who made his living waylaying unsuspecting travelers. He tied everyone who fell into his grasp to an iron bed. If they were longer than the bed, he cut short their legs to make their bodies fit; if they were shorter, he stretched their bodies until they fit tightly. Hence, "procrustean" means *tending to produce conformity through violent or arbitrary means.*

Test 1: True/False

In the space provided, write T if the definition of the numbered word is true or F if it is false.

			T or F
1.	PROCRUSTEAN	marine life	_____
2.	PECUNIARY	picayune	_____
3.	PRECIPITATE	play	_____
4.	PRETEXT	falsification	_____
5.	PARIAH	outcast	_____
6.	POPLIN	religious vestment	_____
7.	PALAVER	serving tray	_____
8.	PRECOCIOUS	advanced	_____
9.	PANNIER	basket	_____
10.	PHANTAS-MAGORIA	illusions	_____

Answers: 1. F   2. F   3. F   4. T   5. T
6. F   7. F   8. T   9. T   10. T

Test 2: Matching Synonyms

Match each of the following numbered words with its closest synonym from the list of lettered words in the second column. Write your answer in the space provided.

1. POPLIN	a. excuse	_____
2. PALAVER	b. producing conformity by violent means	_____
3. PECUNIARY	c. fabric	_____
4. PHANTAS-MAGORIA	d. fantasy	_____
5. PRETEXT	e. expedite	_____
6. PRECOCIOUS	f. idle chatter	_____
7. PRECIPITATE	g. advanced	_____
8. PARIAH	h. outcast	_____
9. PROCRUSTEAN	i. basket	_____
10. PANNIER	j. monetary	_____

Answers: 1. c   2. f   3. j   4. d   5. a
6. g   7. e   8. h   9. b   10. i

LESSON 3 🕐

Read through the interesting stories behind these ten words. Then work through the two self-tests to see how many of the words you can use correctly.

1. **proletariat** (prō'li târ'ē ət)
"Proletariat" derives from the Latin "proletarius," *a Roman freeman who lacked property and money*. The word came from "proles," *offspring, children*. Although the freemen had the vote, many wealthy Romans despised them, saying they were useful only to have children. They called them "proletarii," *producers of children*. Karl

Marx picked up the word in the mid-nineteenth century as a label for the lower-class working people of his age. "Proletariat" retains the same meaning today: *members of the working class, especially those who do not possess capital and must sell their labor to survive.*

2. **Arcadian** (är kā′dē ən)

The residents of landlocked Arcadia, in ancient Greece, did not venture to other lands. As a result, they maintained traditional ways and lived what others imagined to be a simpler life. Ancient classical poets made "Arcadia" a symbol for a land of pastoral happiness. In the sixteenth century, English poet Sir Philip Sidney referred to a bucolic land he called "Arcadia." The word has retained this meaning, and today we consider residents of an "Arcadian" place to be *rustic, simple, and innocent.*

3. **rake** (rāk)

"Rake," meaning *a dissolute person, especially a man,* was originally "rakehell." In the sixteenth century, this colorful term was used to describe a person so dissipated that he would "rake hell" to find his pleasures. "Rakehell" is now considered a somewhat archaic term to describe such roués; "rake" is the common word.

4. **pygmy** (pig′mē)

The ancient Greeks were entranced by stories of a tribe of dwarfs in the upper Nile who were so small that they could be swallowed by cranes. To describe these tiny people, the Greeks used the word "pygmaios," which also referred to the distance on a person's arm from the elbow to the knuckles. The word became English "pygmy," *a tiny person or thing; a person or thing of small importance.*

5. **sardonic** (sär don′ik)

The ancient Greeks described a plant on the island of Sardinia whose flesh, if eaten, caused the victim's face to become grotesquely convulsed, as if in scornful laughter. The Greek name for Sardinia was "Sardos"; therefore, "sardonios" came to refer to any mocking laughter. The English word eventually became "sardonic," *characterized by bitter irony or scornful derision.*

6. **tartar** (tär′tər)

The fierce Genghis Khan and his successors led an army of bloodthirsty warriors, including the Ta-ta Mongols, in a series of conquests throughout Asia and into Europe. Their name, "Tartar" or "Tatar," became closely associated with brutal massacres. Today the word "tartar" refers to *a savage, ill-tempered, or intractable person.*

7. **argosy** (är′gə sē)

In the Middle Ages, cities on the Mediterranean coast maintained large fleets to ship goods around the known world. Ragusa was a Sicilian city well known for its large ships, called "ragusea." In English, the initial two letters became switched, creating "argusea." From there it was a short step to "argosy," *a large merchant ship, especially one with a rich cargo.* Because of Ragusa's wealth, the word "argosy" also came to mean *an opulent supply or collection.*

8. **Balkanize** (bôl′kə nīz′)
After centuries of war, in 1912 the Balkan nations united to conquer the Turks and divide the spoils among themselves. The following year, however, the Balkan nations quarreled over how to divide their booty and began to fight among themselves. From this experience comes the verb "Balkanize," *to divide a country or territory into small, quarrelsome, ineffectual states.*

9. **cravat** (krə vat′)
In the late seventeenth century, the French king Louis XIV formed a special division of Croats, a Slavic people, to serve in his army. The Croats wore colorful, much-admired neckties to distinguish themselves from the other regiments. Fashionable civilians took to wearing these neckties, calling them "cravats" after a variant spelling of "Croat." The term is still used to mean *necktie,* although it is somewhat out of fashion. It also refers to a scarf worn by men.

10. **hegira** (hi jī′rə, hej′ər ə)
Around the year 600, the prophet Muhammad began to preach the new faith of Islam.

To escape persecution, he was forced to flee his home in Mecca. Eventually, his followers increased, and by his death in 632, he controlled Arabia. Within a century, the empire of Islam had spread throughout western Asia and northern Africa. The turning point, Muhammad's flight from Mecca, came to be called the "Hegira," after the Arabic word for *flight* or *emigration*. The "Hegira" is the starting point on the Muslim calendar, and we now apply the word to *any flight or journey to a desirable or congenial place.*

Test 1: True/False

In the space provided, write T if the definition of the numbered word is true or F if it is false.

			T or F
1.	RAKE	roué	_____
2.	PROLETARIAT	wealthy persons	_____
3.	HEGIRA	flight	_____
4.	CRAVAT	craving	_____
5.	TARTAR	disciple	_____
6.	ARCADIAN	rustic	_____
7.	SARDONIC	derisive	_____
8.	PYGMY	monkey	_____
9.	ARGOSY	rich supply	_____
10.	BALKANIZE	vulcanize	_____

Answers: 1. T   2. F   3. T   4. F   5. F
6. T   7. T   8. F   9. T   10. F

Test 2: Matching Synonyms

Select the best definition for each numbered word. Write your answer in the space provided.

1. RAKE	a. bucolic	___
2. PYGMY	b. merchant ship	___
3. CRAVAT	c. midget	___
4. ARCADIAN	d. break up into antagonistic units	___
5. ARGOSY	e. the working class	___
6. HEGIRA	f. scornful; mocking	___
7. BALKANIZE	g. necktie	___
8. PROLETARIAT	h. bad-tempered person	___
9. SARDONIC	i. journey or flight	___
10. TARTAR	j. roué	___

Answers: 1. j   2. c   3. g   4. a   5. b
6. i   7. d   8. e   9. f   10. h

LESSON 4 🕐

Now look at the backgrounds of these ten words. Then complete the two self-tests to help you add them to your vocabulary.

1. **ballyhoo** (bal′ē hōō′)
   The word "ballyhoo" is of uncertain origin. Some, however, have connected it with the Irish town of Ballyhooy, known for the rowdy

and often uncontrolled quarrels of its inhabitants. Today "ballyhoo" is an Americanism with a specific meaning: *a clamorous attempt to win customers or advance a cause; blatant advertising or publicity.*

2. **tawdry** (tô′drē)

In the seventh century, an Englishwoman named Etheldreda fled her husband to establish an abbey. When the Venerable Bede recounted her story in the early eighth century, he claimed that her death had been caused by a tumor in her throat, which she believed was a punishment for her early vanity of wearing jewelry about her neck. Her abbey eventually became the Cathedral of Ely; her name, Audrey. In her honor, the cathedral town held an annual fair where "trifling objects" were hawked. One theory as to the development of the word "tawdry" relates to the hawkers' cry, "Saint Audrey's lace!" This became "Sin t'Audrey lace" and then "tawdry lace." By association with these cheap trinkets, the word "tawdry" has come to mean *gaudy, showy,* or *cheap.*

3. **python** (pī′thon)

According to Greek myth, the sacred oracle at Delphi was at one time threatened by a terrible serpent called "Python." It was finally killed by Apollo. About 150 years ago, *a large constrictor snake often measuring more than twenty feet long* was named after this mythical monster.

4. **recalcitrant** (ri kal'si trənt)

The word was formed from the Latin prefix "re-," *back*, and "calcitrare," *to kick*. Thus, a recalcitrant person is one who kicks back, resisting authority or control.

5. **copperhead** (kop'ər hed')

The term "copperhead" was coined by the New York *Tribune* in the early days of the Civil War to refer to *a Northerner who sympathized with the South*. The term came from the sneaky and poisonous copperhead snake, which strikes without warning.

6. **silhouette** (sil'o͞o et')

At the urging of his mistress, Madame de Pompadour, the French king Louis XV appointed Étienne de Silhouette as his finance minister. His mission was to enact strict economy measures to rescue the government from near-bankruptcy. At the same time, there was a revival of the practice of tracing profiles created by shadows. Since they replaced more costly paintings, these outlines came to be derided as "à la Silhouette"—another of his money-saving measures. Although Silhouette lasted in office less than a year, he achieved a sort of immortality when his name became permanently associated with *a two-dimensional representation of the outline of an object, as a person's profile, generally filled in with black*.

7. **remora** (rem′ər ə)

Since this odd fish impeded the progress of Roman ships by attaching itself to the vessels with its sucking disks, the Romans named it a "remora," *that which holds back; hindrance.* Today we use the term only to name the fish, though formerly it was also a synonym for *obstacle, hindrance.*

8. **caprice** (kə prēs′)

"Caprice," *a sudden, unpredictable change of mind, a whim,* doesn't remind us of hedgehogs, yet these animals probably played a role in this word's past. "Caprice" comes ultimately from the Italian word "capriccio," which originally meant *fright, horror.* The word is thought to be a compound of "capo," *head,* and "riccio," *hedgehog,* because when people are very frightened, their hair stands on end, like a hedgehog's spines.

9. **treacle** (trē′kəl)

Originally, "treacle" was an ointment used by the ancient Romans and Greeks against the bite of wild animals. But in the eighteenth and nineteenth centuries, competing quack medicine hawkers added sweetening to make their bitter potions more palatable. After a while, the sweetening agent itself, usually molasses, came to be called "treacle." We retain this meaning and have extended it to refer figuratively to *contrived or unrestrained sentimentality* as well.

10. **billingsgate** (bil′ingz gāt′)

In the 1500s, "Belin's gate," a walled town within London, was primarily a fish market. The name was soon distorted to "billingsgate," and since many fishwives and seamen were known for their salty tongues, the word "billingsgate" came to mean *coarse or vulgar abusive language*.

Test 1: True/False

In the space provided, write T if the definition of the numbered word is true or F if it is false.

			T or F
1.	RECALCITRANT	easygoing	_____
2.	CAPRICE	capable	_____
3.	REMORA	renovate	_____
4.	COPPERHEAD	fierce warrior	_____
5.	BALLYHOO	dance	_____
6.	TAWDRY	gaudy	_____
7.	BILLINGSGATE	profane language	_____
8.	PYTHON	snake	_____
9.	TREACLE	sugar	_____
10.	SILHOUETTE	outline	_____

Answers: 1. F 2. F 3. F 4. F 5. F
6. T 7. T 8. T 9. F 10. T

Test 2: Matching Synonyms

Match each of the following numbered words with its closest synonym. Write your answer in the space provided.

1.	PYTHON	a.	whim	_____
2.	BALLYHOO	b.	cheap	_____
3.	TREACLE	c.	verbal abuse	_____
4.	TAWDRY	d.	snake	_____
5.	COPPERHEAD	e.	outline	_____
6.	RECALCITRANT	f.	clamor	_____
7.	SILHOUETTE	g.	balky	_____
8.	CAPRICE	h.	mawkish sentimentality	_____
9.	REMORA	i.	fish	_____
10.	BILLINGSGATE	j.	Southern sympathizer	_____

Answers: 1. d   2. f   3. h   4. b   5. j
6. g   7. e   8. a   9. i   10. c

LESSON 5 🕐

The stories behind these ten words provide intriguing reading and can give your vocabulary true power. After you study the words, complete the two self-tests to see how many of the words you can use correctly.

1. **apartheid** (ə pärt′hāt, -hīt)
"Apartheid," the term for *a policy of racial segregation and discrimination against non-whites*, entered English from Afrikaans, the language of South Africa's Dutch settlers, the Boers. They created the word from the Dutch word for "apart" and the suffix

"-heid," related to our suffix "-hood." Thus, the word literally means *apartness* or *separateness*. It was first used in 1947, in a South African newspaper.

2. **quixotic** (kwik sot′ik)
   The word "quixotic," meaning *extravagantly chivalrous or romantic,* is based on the character of Don Quixote, the chivalrous knight in Cervantes' 1605 masterpiece *Don Quixote de la Mancha.* The impractical, visionary knight was ludicrously blind to the false nature of his dreams.

3. **bromide** (brō′mīd)
   "Bromides" are chemicals, several of which can be used as sedatives. In 1906, the American humorist Gelett Burgess first used the word to mean *a boring person,* one who is likely to serve the same purpose as a sedative. The term was then extended to mean *a platitude,* the kind of remark one could expect from a tiresome person.

4. **profane** (prə fān′, prō-)
   Only fully initiated men were allowed to participate in Greek and Roman religious rites; those not admitted were called "profane," from "pro," *outside,* and "fanum," *temple.* When the word came into English, it was applied to persons or things not part of Christianity. Probably in reference to the contempt of nonbelievers, "profane" now means *characterized by irreverence for God or sacred things.*

5. **rialto** (rē al'tō)

In the late sixteenth century, the Venetians erected a bridge across the Grand Canal. Since the bridge spanned deep waters, it was called the "Rialto," *deep stream*. The bridge led to the creation of a busy shopping area in the center of the city. From this shopping center we derive our present meaning of "rialto," *an exchange or mart*.

6. **thespian** (thes'pē ən)

A Greek poet named Thespis, who flourished circa 534 B.C., enlarged the traditional celebrations at the festival of Dionysus by writing verses to be chanted alternately by individuals and the chorus. This opportunity to be a solo performer was a first. From the poet's name we derive the word "thespian," *an actor or actress*.

7. **salver** (sal'vər)

"Salver" came into English from Spanish "salva," a kind of tray. The Spanish word derived from Latin "salvare," *to save*, from the practice of having a servant taste one's food or drink to check for poison. Because poisoning was the method of choice for eliminating wealthy enemies in the Middle Ages, the practice of retaining a taster was commonplace among the affluent. The master's food was presented upon a separate tray, so the term "salva" came to apply to the tray as well as the tasting. Once the habit of poisoning people subsided, the English term "salver" came to mean *a tray, especially one used for serving food.*

8. **chagrin** (shə grin′)

The word "chagrin," meaning *a feeling of vexation due to disappointment,* does not derive from "shagreen," *a piece of hard, abrasive leather used to polish metal,* even though both words are spelled identically in French. French scholars connect "chagrin," *vexation, grief,* with an Old French verb, "chagreiner," *to turn melancholy or gloomy,* which evolved in part from a Germanic word related to English "grim."

9. **shibboleth** (shib′ə lith, -leth′)

In the twelfth chapter of Judges, Jephthah and his men were victorious over the warriors of Ephraim. After the battle, Jephthah gave his guards the password "shibboleth" to distinguish friends from foes; he picked the word because the Ephraimites could not pronounce the "sh" sound. His choice was shrewd, and many of his enemies were captured and killed. Thus, "shibboleth" has come to mean *a peculiarity of pronunciation, usage, or behavior that distinguishes a particular class or set of persons.* It also can mean *slogan; catchword.*

10. **vie** (vī)

The word "vie," *to strive in competition or rivalry with another, to contend for superiority,* was originally a shortened version of "envien," *a sixteenth-century gaming term* meaning *to raise the stake*. The contraction, "vie," came to mean *to contend, compete*.

Test 1: True/False

In the space provided, write T if the definition of the numbered word is true or F if it is false.

			T or F
1. CHAGRIN	chafe		_____
2. VIE	accede		_____
3. PROFANE	irreverent		_____
4. SALVER	tray		_____
5. QUIXOTIC	ill-tempered		_____
6. RIALTO	marketplace		_____
7. APARTHEID	foreigner		_____
8. SHIBBOLETH	platitude		_____
9. THESPIAN	actor		_____
10. BROMIDE	explosive		_____

Answers: 1. F   2. F   3. T   4. T   5. F
6. T   7. F   8. F   9. T   10. F

Test 2: Definitions

Select the best definition for each numbered word. Circle your answer.

1. BROMIDE
   a. cliché   b. effervescence   c. angst
2. VIE
   a. treat   b. contend   c. despise

3. QUIXOTIC
   a. alien   b. romantic   c. fictional
4. SALVER
   a. salivate   b. poison   c. tray
5. SHIBBOLETH
   a. peculiarity   b. forbidden   c. murdered
6. PROFANE
   a. pious   b. irreverent   c. exploding
7. THESPIAN
   a. actress   b. speech impairment
            c. playwright
8. APARTHEID
   a. discrimination   b. unity   c. hopelessness
9. RIALTO
   a. shipyard   b. reality   c. exchange
10. CHAGRIN
   a. stiff   b. vexation   c. smirk

Answers: 1. a   2. b   3. b   4. c   5. a
6. b   7. a   8. a   9. c   10. b

LESSON 6 🕐

Knowing the histories of the following ten words can help you remember their meanings and use them in your speech and writing. Study the words, then work through the two tests that follow.

1. **Promethean** (prə mē'thē ən)
   According to Greek myth, as punishment for stealing fire from the gods and giving it to

mortal humans, Prometheus was bound to the side of a mountain, where he was attacked daily by a fierce bird that feasted upon his liver. At night his wounds healed; the next day he was attacked anew. Because of his extraordinary boldness in stealing the divine fire, the word "Promethean" has come to mean *creative, boldly original.*

2. **sarcophagus** (sär kof′ə gəs)
   Although the majority of ancient Greeks favored burial or cremation, some obtained limestone coffins that could dissolve a body in little over a month. The coffin was called a "sarcophagus," from the Greek "sarx," *flesh,* and "phagos," *eating.* Today we use the term to refer to *a stone coffin, especially one bearing sculpture, an inscription, etc., often displayed as a monument.*

3. **quorum** (kwôr′əm)
   The word "quorum" was first used as part of a Latin phrase meaning *to select people for official court business.* Ultimately, it came to mean *the number of members of a group or organization required to be present to transact business; legally, usually a majority.*

4. **antimacassar** (an′ti mə kas′ər)
   In the 1800s, macassar oil was imported from Indonesia to England as a popular remedy for baldness. Based on its reputation, men began to apply it liberally to their pates, but the oil stained the backs of sofas and chairs where they rested their oily heads.

Therefore, homemakers began to place pieces of fabric over sofa and chair backs, since these scraps could be washed more easily than stained upholstery. These fabric pieces came to be called "antimacassars"— *against macassar oil*. They survive today in the *little doilies* fastidious homemakers drape over furniture.

5. **lackey** (lak'ē)

After their invasion of Spain in 711, the Moors conquered nearly the entire country and established a glittering civilization. But it was not to last. By 1100, Christians had already wrested half of Spain from the Moors. Two hundred years later, the Moors retained only a small toehold; and a hundred years after that, they were driven out of Europe entirely. As the Moors suffered repeated defeats, their captured soldiers became servants to their Spanish conquerors. They were called "alacayo." The initial "a" was later dropped, and the word was rendered in English as "lackey," *a servile follower*.

6. **obelisk** (ob'ə lisk')

The word comes from the ancient Egyptian practice of erecting tall, thin pillars to pay homage to the sun god Ra. The Greeks called these shafts "obeliskoi." The word has come down to us as "obelisk," with its meaning intact, *a tapering four-sided shaft of stone with a pyramidal apex; a monument.*

7. **paladin** (pal'ə din)

The original paladins were Charlemagne's twelve knights. According to legend, the famous paladin Roland was caught in an ambush and fought valiantly with his small band of followers to the last man. Because of his actions, "paladin" has come down to us as *any champion of noble causes*.

8. **hobnob** (hob'nob')

Those who "hobnob" with their buddies *associate on very friendly terms* or *drink together*. The word comes from the Anglo-Saxon "haebbe" and "naebbe," *to have* and *to have not*. In the 1700s, "hobnob" meant *to toast friends and host alternate rounds of drinks*. Each person thus had the pleasure of treating, creating a sense of familiarity. Today this usage survives, even if those hobnobbing are teetotalers.

9. **helot** (hel'ət, hē'lət)

Around the eighth century B.C., the Spartans conquered and enslaved the people of the southern half of the Peloponnesus. They called these slaves "helots," perhaps from the Greek word meaning *to enslave*. Today "helot" still means *serf or slave; bondsman*.

10. **kowtow** (kou'tou')

The Chinese people, who were largely isolated from the West until Portuguese traders established a post outside Canton, regarded their emperor as a representation of God on earth. Those approaching the emperor had to fall to the ground and strike their heads against the floor as a sign of humility. This was called a "kowtow," from the Chinese word that meant *knock-head*. As a verb, the English word follows the original meaning, *to touch the forehead to the ground while kneeling, as an act of worship;* but from this meaning we have derived a figurative use as well: *to act in an obsequious manner; show servile deference.*

Test 1: Defining Words

Define each of the following words.

1. obelisk _____
2. Promethean _____
3. helot _____
4. sarcophagus _____
5. kowtow _____
6. lackey _____
7. antimacassar _____
8. hobnob _____
9. quorum _____
10. paladin _____

Suggested Answers: 1. shaft 2. creative, boldly original 3. serf, slave 4. coffin 5. deference 6. a servile follower 7. doily 8. associate on friendly terms; drink together 9. majority 10. champion

Test 2: True/False

In the space provided, write T if the definition of the numbered word is true or F if it is false.

		T or F
1. LACKEY	servant	_____
2. QUORUM	majority	_____
3. OBELISK	shaft	_____
4. HOBNOB	twisted logic	_____
5. PROMETHEAN	creative	_____
6. SARCOPHAGUS	cremation	_____
7. HELOT	hell-on-wheels	_____
8. ANTIMACASSAR	against travel	_____
9. KOWTOW	bow low	_____
10. PALADIN	villain	_____

Answers: 1. T   2. T   3. T   4. F   5. T
6. F   7. F   8. F   9. T   10. F

LESSON 7 ⏰

The quirky stories behind the following ten words can help you understand and remember them better. Read through the histories and complete the two self-tests to add to your mastery of language.

1. **quahog** (kwô′hôg, -hog)
   Despite the "hog" at the end of the word, a "quahog" has nothing to do with a pig. Rather, it is a clam; the word comes from

the Algonquian (Narragansett) word "poquauhock."

2. **protean** (prō'tē ən)

According to Greek legend, Proteus was a sea god who possessed the power to change his shape at will. He also had the ability to foretell the future, but those wishing to avail themselves of his power first had to steal upon him at noon when he checked his herds of sea calves, catch him, and bind him securely. Thus bound, Proteus would change shape furiously, but the petitioner who could keep him restrained until he returned to his original shape would receive the answer to his question—if he still remembered what he wanted to know. From Proteus, then, we get the word "protean," *readily assuming different forms or characters; variable.*

3. **noisome** (noi'səm)

Although the words appear to have the same root, "noisome" bears no relation to "noise." "Noisome" means *offensive* or *disgusting,* as an odor, and comes from the Middle English word "noy," meaning *harm.* The root is related, however, to the word "annoy," *to molest or bother.*

4. **Ouija** (wē'jə)

"Ouija" is a trademark for *a board game used to spell out messages in spiritualistic communication.* It consists of a small board, or planchette, resting on a larger board marked with words and letters. The name comes from the French and German words for *yes*, "oui" and "ja."

5. **simony** (sī′mə nē, sim′ə-)
Simon the sorcerer offered to pay the Apostle Peter to teach him the wondrous cures he had seen him perform, not understanding that his feats were miracles rather than magic tricks. From Simon's name comes the term "simony," *the sin of buying or selling ecclesiastical preferments.*

6. **rigmarole** (rig′mə rōl′)
In fourteenth-century England, a register of names was called a "rageman." Later it became a "ragman," then "ragman roll." As it changed, the term evolved to refer to a series of unconnected statements. By the 1700s, the word had become "rigmarole," with its present meaning, *an elaborate or complicated procedure.*

7. **bolshevik** (bōl′shə vik)
At a rally of Communist leaders in 1903, Lenin garnered a majority of the votes. He cleverly dubbed his supporters "Bolsheviks," meaning *the majority*. His move was effective propaganda. Even though his supporters actually comprised only a minority, the name stuck and came to be associated with *a member of the Russian Communist party*. The word is also used in a derogatory sense to denote *an extreme political radical, a revolutionary.*

8. **misericord** (miz′ər i kôrd′, mi zer′i kôrd′)

Both the *small projection on the underside of a hinged seat of a church stall that gives support, when the seat is lifted, to a person standing in the stall* and *a medieval dagger* have the same name, "misericord." In a curious sense, this is because they both provide mercy, the seat giving a parishioner a resting place during a long service, the dagger delivering the coup de grâce to a wounded foe. "Misericord" comes from the Latin "misericordia," meaning *compassion.*

9. **surplice** (sûr′plis)

To keep themselves warm in damp, chilly stone churches, clergymen in the Middle Ages wore fur robes. But since fur was not considered proper attire for religious men, the priests covered their furs with loose-fitting white overgarments. The word "surplice" to describe these broad-sleeved white vestments came from their function: the Latin "super," *over,* and "pellicia," *fur garment.*

10. **sylph** (silf)

A German alchemist of the 1700s coined the term "Sylphis" to describe the spirits of the air. He envisioned them as looking like humans but able to move more swiftly and gracefully. Over the years, the word evolved to mean *a slender, graceful girl or woman.*

Test 1: True/False

In the space provided, write T if the definition of the numbered word is true or F if it is false.

			T or F
1.	MISERICORD	wretchedness	———
2.	OUIJA	board game	———
3.	SIMONY	slickness	———
4.	BOLSHEVIK	sheik	———
5.	PROTEAN	changeable	———
6.	NOISOME	clamorous	———
7.	SYLPH	svelte female	———
8.	QUAHOG	bivalve	———
9.	RIGMAROLE	simplification	———
10.	SURPLICE	clerical vestment	———

Answers: 1. F 2. T 3. F 4. F 5. T
6. F 7. T 8. T 9. F 10. T

Test 2: Matching Synonyms

Match each of the numbered words with its closest synonym from the list of lettered words in the second column. Write your answer in the space provided.

1. SYLPH	a. vestment	_____
2. QUAHOG	b. medieval dagger	_____
3. SURPLICE	c. ecclesiastical favors	_____
4. BOLSHEVIK	d. slender girl	_____
5. OUIJA	e. Communist	_____
6. MISERICORD	f. involved process	_____
7. NOISOME	g. variable	_____
8. PROTEAN	h. clam	_____
9. RIGMAROLE	i. foul	_____
10. SIMONY	j. board game	_____

Answers: 1. d 2. h 3. a 4. e 5. j
6. b 7. i 8. g 9. f 10. c

LESSON 8 🕐

Now read the histories of these ten unique words. Fix them in your memory by completing the two self-tests that follow. The words can make your speech and writing more colorful, interesting, and effective.

1. **muumuu** (moo͞′moo͞′)
   This *loose dress, often brightly colored or patterned,* was first introduced into Hawaii by missionaries anxious to clothe their nude Hawaiian female converts. To accomplish their aims, the missionaries gave the Hawaiian women dresses cut in the European fashion, which the Hawaiians adapted to suit their needs and climate. The dress

acquired the Hawaiian name "muumuu," which means *cut off*, because it lacked a yoke and therefore looked "cut off" at the neck.

2. **sybarite** (sib'ə rīt')

The ancient Greek colony of Sybaris in southern Italy was known for its luxurious life style. The residents were so famous for their opulent ways that the word "sybarite" came to be used for *any person devoted to luxury and pleasure*.

3. **rostrum** (ros'trəm)

Today a "rostrum" is *any platform, stage, or the like for public speaking*. The word comes from the victory in 338 B.C. of the Romans over the pirates of Antium (Anzio), off the Italian coast. The victorious consul took back to Rome the prows of the six ships he had captured. These were attached to the lecterns used by Roman speakers. They came to be called "rostra," or *beaks*. We use the singular, "rostrum."

4. **lemur** (lē'mər)

An animal with a small foxlike face, woolly fur, and cute monkeylike body, the "lemur" seems to some people to be an adorable creature. The scientist who first named this small nocturnal mammal, the eighteenth-century Swedish botanist Linnaeus, obviously had a less pleasant reaction to the animal, since the Latin word "lemur" denotes *malevolent, frightening spirits of the dead*.

5. **spoonerism** (spo͞o'nə riz'əm)
The English clergyman W. A. Spooner (1844–1930) was notorious for his habit of transposing the initial letters or other sounds of words, as in "a blushing crow" for "a crushing blow." Since the good reverend was not unique in his affliction, we use the word "spoonerism" to describe these *unintentional transpositions of sounds*.

6. **vermicelli** (vûr'mi chel'ē)
Anyone faced with a small child determined not to eat his or her spaghetti because "it looks like worms" had better avoid explaining the origin of "vermicelli." In Italian, "vermicelli" is the plural of "vermicello," a diminutive of "verme," which does indeed mean *worm*. When dealing with recalcitrant children, it's probably better to refer to these *long, slender threads of spaghetti* simply as "pasta."

7. **pundit** (pun'dit)
Today we use the word "pundit" to mean *an expert or authority;* but in the nineteenth century, the word was usually applied to a learned person in India. It comes from the Hindi word "pandit," meaning *learned man*, a Brahman with profound knowledge of Sanskrit, Hindu law, and so forth.

8. **yahoo** (yä'ho͞o)
This word for a *coarse, uncouth person* was coined by Jonathan Swift in his 1726 novel *Gulliver's Travels*. In Swift's satire, the

Yahoos were a race of humanoid brutes ruled by the Houyhnhnms, civilized horses.

9. **stoic** (stō′ik)

The Stoics were philosophers of ancient Greece who believed in self-restraint. Their name comes from Greek *stoa*, "porch," where they habitually walked. Hence the word "stoic," which describes a person who is *impassive, calm, and austere*.

10. **wormwood** (wûrm′wŏŏd′)

"Wormwood" is the active narcotic ingredient of absinthe, a bitter green liqueur now banned in most Western countries. Originally, however, the herb was used as a folk remedy for worms in the body. Because of the herb's bitter qualities, we also use it figuratively to mean *something bitter, grievous, or extremely unpleasant*.

Test 1: True/False

In the space provided, write T if the definition of the numbered word is true or F if it is false.

			T or F
1.	SPOONERISM	Midwesterner	____
2.	YAHOO	oaf	____
3.	WORMWOOD	bitterness	____
4.	MUUMUU	murmur	____
5.	PUNDIT	bad kick	____
6.	LEMUR	monkeylike nocturnal mammal	____

			T or F
7. SYBARITE	slender		_____
8. STOIC	austere		_____
9. VERMICELLI	aggravation		_____
10. ROSTRUM	register		_____

Answers: 1. F   2. T   3. T   4. F   5. F
6. T   7. F   8. T   9. F   10. F

Test 2: Matching Synonyms

Select the best definition for each numbered word. Write your answer in the space provided.

1. ROSTRUM	a. loose dress	_____
2. YAHOO	b. something bitter	_____
3. MUUMUU	c. small nocturnal mammal	_____
4. SPOONERISM	d. long, thin threadlike pasta	_____
5. WORMWOOD	e. impassive	_____
6. SYBARITE	f. stage or platform	_____
7. LEMUR	g. authority	_____
8. PUNDIT	h. lover of luxury	_____
9. VERMICELLI	i. transposition of sounds in words	_____
10. STOIC	j. boor	_____

Answers: 1. f   2. j   3. a   4. i   5. b
6. h   7. c   8. g   9. d   10. e

LESSON 9 🕐

Here are ten more words with intriguing pasts.
Read through the histories, then complete the
self-tests that follow. Spend a few minutes using each of the words in a sentence to help you
make them part of your everyday speech and
writing.

1. **termagant** (tûr′mə gənt)
   The word "termagant," meaning *a violent,
   turbulent, or brawling woman,* comes from a
   mythical deity that many Europeans of the
   Middle Ages believed was worshiped by the
   Muslims. It often appeared in morality plays
   as a violent, overbearing personage in long
   robes. In modern usage, "termagant" is applied only to women.

2. **blarney** (blär′nē)
   According to Irish legend, anyone who kisses
   a magical stone set twenty feet beneath the
   ground of a castle near the village of Blarney,
   in Ireland, will henceforth possess the gift of
   eloquence. One story claims the Blarney
   Stone got its powers from the eloquence of
   the seventeenth-century Irish patriot Cor-
   mac McCarthy, whose soft speech won favorable terms from Elizabeth I after an Irish
   uprising. From this stone-kissing custom,
   "blarney" has come to mean *flattering or
   wheedling talk; cajolery.*

3. **schooner** (skōō′nər)

According to legend, Captain Andrew Robinson built the first "schooner," *a sailing vessel with a foremast and a mainmast.* As it cut smoothly into the water on its maiden voyage, someone presumably was heard to exclaim, "Oh, how she scoons!" Picking up on the praise, Robinson decided to call his previously unnamed ship a "scooner." The "h" was added later. Scholars, however, doubt the veracity of this story and regard the word's source as uncertain.

4. **eunuch** (yōō′nək)

A "eunuch" is *a castrated man,* especially formerly, one employed by Oriental rulers as a harem attendant. The word is based on the Greek "eunouchos," from "eune," *bed,* and "echein," *to keep,* since a eunuch is perfectly suited for guarding a woman's bed. The word is used figuratively to refer to *a weak, powerless person.*

5. **reefer** (rē′fər)

The word "reefer" has several different meanings; but in the nineteenth century, the word was used to refer to sailors. The term came from a description of their duties, the taking in of the reefs. Heavy woolen coats hindered the seamen in the execution of their duties, so they wore close-fitting coats instead. These coats took their name from the sailors who wore them, and today we often refer to *any short coat or jacket of thick cloth* as a "reefer."

6. **shrew** (shrōō)

In Old English, the word "shrew" described *a small, fierce rodent*. The word was later applied to *a person with a violent temper and tenacious personality* similar to the rodent's. Although "shrew" has retained this meaning, it is usually applied only to a woman.

7. **kudos** (kōō′dōz, kyōō′-)

Although "kudos" has come down to us from the Greek intact in both form and meaning—*praise, glory*—in the process it has come to be regarded as a plural word, although it is singular. As a result, another new word has been formed, "kudo." Although purists still prefer "kudos is" to "kudos are," only time will tell if the transformation to kudo/kudos becomes permanent.

8. **bohemian** (bō hē′mē ən)

In the early fifteenth century, a band of vagabond peasants took up residence in Paris. Knowing that they had come from somewhere in central Europe, the French dubbed the gypsies "Bohemians," in the belief that they were natives of Bohemia. Working from the stereotyped view of gypsies as free spirits, the French then applied the term "bohemian" to *a person, typically one with artistic or intellectual aspirations, who lives an unconventional life*.

9. **rhubarb** (roo′bärb)

In conventional usage, the word refers to *a long-stalked plant*, used in tart conserves and pie fillings; it is also a slang term for *quarrel* or *squabble*. The ancient Greeks gave the plant its name. Since it grew in an area outside of Greece, they called it "rha barbaron." "Rha" was the name of the plant and "barbaron" meant *foreign*.

10. **lacuna** (lə kyoo′nə)

"Lacuna," *a gap or missing part; hiatus*, comes from the identical Latin word, "lacuna," meaning *a hollow*. It first entered English to refer to a missing part in a manuscript. It is also the root of "lagoon."

Test 1: True/False

In the space provided, write T if the definition of the numbered word is true or F if it is false.

			T or F
1.	KUDOS	compliment	_____
2.	BLARNEY	cajolery	_____
3.	SHREW	cleverness	_____
4.	REEFER	woolen coat	_____
5.	LACUNA	hiatus	_____
6.	TERMAGANT	intermediate	_____
7.	BOHEMIAN	businesslike	_____
8.	SCHOONER	sailing vessel	_____
9.	RHUBARB	sweet	_____
10.	EUNUCH	castrated man	_____

Answers: 1. T 2. T 3. F 4. T 5. T
6. F 7. F 8. T 9. F 10. T

Test 2: Definitions

Select the best definition for each numbered word. Write your answer in the space provided.

_____ 1. KUDOS
    a. enclave   c. acclaim
    b. martial arts d. humiliation

_____ 2. EUNUCH
    a. hero   c. castle
    b. warrior   d. castrated man

_____ 3. BOHEMIAN
    a. free spirit c. foreigner
    b. butcher   d. master chef

_____ 4. SHREW
    a. virago   c. bibliophile
    b. sly   d. hearty

_____ 5. LACUNA
    a. hot tub   c. lake
    b. gap   d. cool water

_____ 6. TERMAGANT
    a. lease   c. possessive
    b. eternal   d. brawling woman

_____ 7. SCHOONER
    a. release   c. possessive
    b. submarine d. sailboat

_____ 8. RHUBARB
    a. root   c. squabble
    b. ridicule   d. arrow

——— 9. BLARNEY
        a. mountain   c. sightseeing
            climbing   d. luncheon meats
        b. sweet talk
——— 10. REEFER
        a. coat   c. exotic fish
        b. renegade   d. regret

Answers: 1. c   2. d   3. a   4. a   5. b
6. d   7. d   8. c   9. b   10. a

LESSON 10 🕐

Recalling the history of these ten words can help you remember their meanings and make them part of your stock of words. Go through the following word histories and complete the self-tests that follow. Then review the histories to help you remember the words.

1. **solecism** (sol′ə siz′əm, sō′lə-)
To the ancient Greeks, the people of the colony of Soloi spoke inexcusably poor Greek. The Greeks were perhaps most offended by the Solois' errors in grammar and usage. They called such barbarous speech "soloikismos," *the language of Soloi.* Through Latin, the word became "solecism," *a substandard or ungrammatical usage; a breech of good manners or etiquette.*

2. **requiem** (rek′wē əm)

A "requiem" is a mass celebrated for the repose of the souls of the dead. It comes from the opening line of the Roman Catholic mass for the dead, "Requiem aeternam dona eis, Domine," meaning *Give them eternal rest, Lord.*

3. **tariff** (tar′if)

"Tariff," *an official schedule of duties or customs imposed by a government on imports and exports,* comes from the Arabic term for *inventory,* "ta'rif." Perhaps because this story is so unexciting, a false etymology claims that the word instead comes from the name of a Moorish town near the straits of Gibraltar formerly used as a base for daring pirate raids. Colorful, but not true.

4. **blitzkrieg** (blits′krēg′)

The German word "Blitzkrieg," literally *a lightning war,* describes the overwhelming Nazi attacks on Poland in 1940. In two weeks, Germany pounded Poland into submission; in six weeks, it crushed the French army. Although ultimately the Germans met defeat, their method of attack has found a place in our language, and "blitzkrieg" has come to denote *an overwhelming, all-out attack.*

5. **entrepreneur** (än′trə prə nûr′, -noŏr′, -nyoŏr′)

"Entrepreneur" came from the French word derived from the verb "entreprendre," *to undertake*. It was initially used in English to denote a musician's manager, the person responsible for such things as organizing concerts; in the nineteenth century, the word assumed its present meaning: *a person who organizes, manages, and assumes responsibility for a business or other enterprise.*

6. **spinnaker** (spin'ə kər)

According to one story, in the mid-nineteenth century, a yachtsman devised a new racing sail. The name of the yacht was the "Sphinx," but the sailors had difficulty pronouncing the word. Their mispronunciation gave us the word "spinnaker," *a large, triangular sail carried by yachts as a headsail when running before the wind.*

7. **reynard** (rā'närd, -nərd, ren'ərd)

This *poetic name given to the fox* comes from the medieval beast epic, stories first circulated orally throughout western Europe, then written down. Aside from countless hours of entertainment, these satirical tales have also provided us with words for other animals: "bruin" for *bear* and "chanticleer" for *rooster.*

8. **kibitzer** (kib'it sər)

A "kibitzer" is *a spectator, especially at a card game, who gives unwanted advice to a player; a meddler.* This word came from Yiddish, which derived it from the German verb "kiebitzen," *to be a busybody; give unwanted advice to card players.* The verb, in turn, came from "Kiebitz," the German word for a lapwing, an inquisitive little bird given to shrill cries.

9. **lampoon** (lam pōon')
"Lampoon," *a sharp, often virulent satire,* comes from the French word "lampon," which is thought to come from "lampons," *let's drink,* a common ending to seventeenth-century French satirical drinking songs. We also use the word as a verb meaning *to mock or ridicule.*

10. **scapegoat** (skāp'gōt')
The term "scapegoat," *a person made to bear the blame for others or to suffer in their place,* comes from the sixteenth chapter of Leviticus, which describes how the high priest Aaron was directed to select two goats. One goat was to be a burnt offering to the Lord; the other, an "escape goat" for atonement, was presented alive to the Lord and sent away into the wilderness to carry away the sins of the people. The word "scape" was a shortening of "escape."

Test 1: True/False

In the space provided, write T if the definition of the numbered word is true or F if it is false.

		T or F
1. KIBITZER	busybody	_____
2. REYNARD	goat	_____

			T or F
3.	BLITZKRIEG	negotiations	———
4.	SOLECISM	bad grammar	———
5.	TARIFF	customs duties	———
6.	SPINNAKER	craftsperson	———
7.	REQUIEM	revival	———
8.	LAMPOON	enlighten	———
9.	SCAPEGOAT	substitute victim	———
10.	ENTREPRENEUR	organizer and manager	———

Answers: 1. T   2. F   3. F   4. T   5. T
6. F   7. F   8. F   9. T   10. T

Test 2: Matching Synonyms

Match each of the following numbered words with its closest synonym. Write your answer in the space provided.

1.	TARIFF	a. sail	———
2.	LAMPOON	b. mock	———
3.	KIBITZER	c. funeral mass	———
4.	SCAPEGOAT	d. fox	———
5.	REYNARD	e. customs duties	———
6.	REQUIEM	f. business manager	———
7.	SOLECISM	g. busybody	———
8.	BLITZKRIEG	h. grammatical error	———
9.	SPINNAKER	i. victim	———
10.	ENTREPRENEUR	j. all-out attack	———

Answers: 1. e   2. b   3. g   4. i   5. d
6. c   7. h   8. j   9. a   10. f

9. IMPORTED WORDS

Along with sushi, crêpes, and pizza—and their names—English has borrowed numerous words from foreign cultures. Here is a selection of "imported" words for you to add to your vocabulary.

LESSON 1 🕐

FRENCH BORROWINGS

We've borrowed so many words from French that someone once half-seriously claimed that English is little more than French badly pronounced. Some of these words have kept their original spelling, while others have become so Anglicized you may not recognize them as originally French.

1. **envoy** (en′voi, än′-) a diplomatic agent; an accredited messenger or representative.
2. **résumé** (rez′oo mā′, rez′oo mā′) a summing up; a brief account of personal, educational, and professional qualifications and experience, as of an applicant for a job.
3. **coup d'état** (koo′dā tä′) a sudden and decisive action in politics, especially one effecting a change of government, illegally or by force.

4. **cause célèbre** (kôz'sə leb', -leb'rə) any controversy that attracts great public attention.

5. **avant-garde** (ə vänt'gärd', ə vant'-, av'än-, ä'vän-) the advance group in any field, especially in the visual, literary, or musical arts, whose works are unorthodox and experimental.

6. **laissez-faire** (les'ā fâr') the theory that government should intervene as little as possible in economic affairs.

7. **rendezvous** (rän'də vōō', -dā-) an agreement between two or more people to meet at a certain time and place.

8. **cul-de-sac** (kul'də sak') a street, lane, etc., closed at one end; blind alley.

9. **esprit de corps** (e sprē'də kôr') a sense of union and of common interests and responsibilities, as developed among a group of persons associated together.

10. **idée fixe** (ē'dā fēks') a fixed idea; obsession.

11. **joie de vivre** (zhwä'də vēv', vē'vrə) a delight in being alive.

12. **milieu** (mil yōō', mēl-) an environment; medium.

13. **potpourri** (pō'pōō rē') a mixture of dried petals of roses or other flowers with spices, kept in a jar for their fragrance.

14. **rapport** (ra pôr', rə-) a harmonious or sympathetic relationship or connection.

15. **bon vivant** (bon'vē vänt', bôn'vē väN') a person who lives luxuriously and enjoys good food and drink.

Test 1: Matching Synonyms

Match each of the following numbered words with its closest synonym. Write your answer in the space provided.

1. RENDEZVOUS	a. togetherness	____
2. RAPPORT	b. experimental artists	____
3. CUL-DE-SAC	c. hands-off policy	____
4. BON VIVANT	d. love of life	____
5. IDÉE FIXE	e. meeting	____
6. JOIE DE VIVRE	f. environment	____
7. POTPOURRI	g. diplomatic agent	____
8. MILIEU	h. harmony	____
9. AVANT-GARDE	i. controversy	____
10. COUP D'ÉTAT	j. government overthrow	____
11. RÉSUMÉ	k. dead end	____
12. ESPRIT DE CORPS	l. list of qualifications	____
13. ENVOY	m. connoisseur	____
14. CAUSE CÉLÈBRE	n. fragrant dried flowers	____
15. LAISSEZ-FAIRE	o. obsession	____

Answers: 1. e   2. h   3. k   4. m   5. o
6. d   7. n   8. f.   9. b   10. j   11. l
12. a   13. g   14. i   15. c

Test 2: True/False

In the space provided, write T if the definition of the numbered word is true or F if it is false.

		T or F
1. LAISSEZ-FAIRE	a policy of leaving alone	_____
2. ESPRIT DE CORPS	harmony and union	_____
3. MILIEU	setting	_____
4. RENDEZVOUS	meeting	_____
5. IDÉE FIXE	obsession	_____
6. POTPOURRI	cooking utensils	_____
7. ENVOY	letter	_____
8. RAPPORT	announcement	_____
9. JOIE DE VIVRE	good vintage	_____
10. COUP D'ÉTAT	headache	_____
11. CAUSE CÉLÈBRE	controversy	_____
12. CUL-DE-SAC	dead end	_____
13. BON VIVANT	good sport	_____
14. RÉSUMÉ	curriculum vitae	_____
15. AVANT-GARDE	front-runners	_____

Answers: 1. T   2. T   3. T   4. T   5. T
6. F   7. F   8. F   9. F   10. F
11. T   12. T   13. T   14. T   15. T

LESSON 2 🕐

ADDITIONAL FRENCH BORROWINGS

Here are fifteen more words borrowed from French. Their mastery can put vigor into your vocabulary, especially in writing.

1. **tour de force** (tōōr'də fôrs') an exceptional achievement using the full skill, ingenuity, and resources of a person, country, or group.

2. **connoisseur** (kon'ə sûr', -sōōr') a person who is especially competent to pass critical judgments in art or in matters of taste.

3. **raconteur** (rak'on tûr', -tōōr') a person who is skilled in relating anecdotes.

4. **poseur** (pō zûr') a person who attempts to impress others by assuming or affecting a manner, degree of elegance, etc.

5. **saboteur** (sab'ə tûr') a person who deliberately destroys property, obstructs services, or undermines a cause.

6. **décolletage** (dā'kol täzh') the neckline of a dress cut low in the front or back and often across the shoulders.

7. **mêlée** (mā'lā, mā lā') a confused, general hand-to-hand fight.

8. **tout à fait** (tōō' tä fā') entirely.

9. **chauffeur** (shō'fər, shō fûr') a person employed to drive another person's automobile.

10. **fiancé** (fē'än sā', fē än'sā) a man engaged to be married.

11. **protégé** (prō'tə zhā', prō'tə zhā') a person under the patronage or care of someone influential who can further his or her career.

12. **gourmet** (gŏŏr mā', gŏŏr'mā) a connoisseur in the delicacies of the table.

13. **tout de suite** (tŏŏt swēt') at once; immediately.

14. **chic** (shēk) attractive and fashionable in style; stylish.

15. **tout le monde** (tŏŏ' lə mônd') everyone; everybody.

Test 1: Defining Words

Define each of the following words.

1. tout à fait _____
2. gourmet _____
3. chauffeur _____
4. tout le monde _____
5. décolletage _____
6. tout de suite _____
7. tour de force _____
8. chic _____
9. protégé _____
10. connoisseur _____
11. raconteur _____
12. mêlée _____
13. saboteur _____
14. poseur _____
15. fiancé _____

Suggested Answers: 1. entirely 2. a connoisseur in the delicacies of the table 3. a person employed to drive another person's automobile 4. everyone; everybody 5. a low-cut neckline or backless dress 6. at once; immediately 7. an exceptional achievement using the full skill, ingenuity, and resources of a person, country, or group 8. attractive and fashionable in style 9. a person under the patronage or care of someone influential who can further his or her career 10. a person who is especially competent to pass critical judgments in art, especially one of the fine arts, or in matters of taste 11. a person who is skilled in relating anecdotes 12. a confused, general hand-to-hand fight 13. a person who destroys property, obstructs services, or subverts a cause 14. a person who attempts to impress others by assuming or affecting a manner, degree of elegance, etc. 15. a man engaged to be married

Test 2: Synonyms

Each of the following phrases contains an italicized word. Select the best synonym for each word from the choices provided. Write your answer in the space provided.

_____ 1. a daring *décolletage*
     a. low-cut dress   c. acrobatics
     b. dance   d. behavior
_____ 2. a *chic* hat
     a. French   c. expensive
     b. imported   d. stylish

_____ 3. the nervous *fiancé*
   a. engaged woman   c. executive
   b. engaged man   d. husband

_____ 4. *tout le monde* attended
   a. connoisseurs   c. everyone
   b. specialists   d. no one

_____ 5. the entertaining *raconteur*
   a. comedian   c. singer
   b. storyteller   d. poet

_____ 6. an amazing *tour de force*
   a. show of force   c. humiliation
   b. war victory   d. achievement

_____ 7. pass the butter *tout de suite*
   a. immediately   c. please
   b. thank you   d. later

_____ 8. a transparent *poseur*
   a. model   c. fraud
   b. prank   d. gag

_____ 9. a captured *saboteur*
   a. spy   c. turncoat
   b. demolisher   d. revolutionary

_____ 10. my *protégé*
   a. mentor   c. child
   b. tutor   d. dependent

_____ 11. a new *chauffeur*
   a. kitchen helper   c. chef
   b. mentor   d. driver

_____ 12. a violent *mêlée*
   a. free-for-all   c. criminal
   b. storm   d. sea

_____ 13. a noted *connoisseur*
   a. expert   c. hostess
   b. politician   d. professor
_____ 14. completed the job *tout à fait*
   a. quickly   c. entirely
   b. sloppily   d. yesterday
_____ 15. a famous *gourmet*
   a. driver   c. heavy eater
   b. waitress   d. food expert

Answers: 1. a   2. d   3. b   4. c   5. b
6. d   7. a   8. c   9. b   10. d
11. d   12. a   13. a   14. c   15. d

LESSON 3 ⏰

Numerous other languages have left their mark
on English as well—including Italian, Spanish,
and Latin. We will begin with a group of words
borrowed from Italian.

ITALIAN BORROWINGS

1. **alfresco** (al fres'kō) out-of-doors; in the
   open air.
2. **piazza** (pē az'ə, -ä'zə) a town square.
3. **dilettante** (dil'i tänt') a person who takes
   up an art, activity, or subject merely for
   amusement; dabbler.
4. **fiasco** (fē as'kō) a complete and ignominious failure.

5. **imbroglio** (im brōl′yō) a confused state of affairs; a complicated or difficult situation; bitter misunderstanding.

6. **impresario** (im′pri sär′ē ō′, -sâr′-) a person who organizes or manages public entertainments; a manager, director, or the like.

7. **incognito** (in′kog nē′tō, in kog′ni tō′) having one's identity concealed, as under an assumed name, especially to avoid notice.

8. **manifesto** (man′ə fes′tō) a public declaration of intentions, opinions, objectives, or motives, as one issued by a government, a sovereign, or an organization.

9. **replica** (rep′li kə) a copy or reproduction of a work of art.

Test 1: Matching Synonyms

Match each of the following numbered words with its closest synonym. Write your answer in the space provided.

1. FIASCO	a. manager	_____
2. IMBROGLIO	b. town square	_____
3. INCOGNITO	c. outdoors	_____
4. IMPRESARIO	d. failure	_____
5. MANIFESTO	e. public declaration	_____
6. PIAZZA	f. confusion	_____
7. REPLICA	g. reproduction	_____
8. ALFRESCO	h. in disguise	_____
9. DILETTANTE	i. dabbler	_____

Answers: 1. d   2. f   3. h   4. a   5. e
6. b   7. g   8. c   9. i

Test 2: Definitions

Each of the following phrases contains an italicized word. From the three choices provided, circle the best definition.

1. an *alfresco* café
   a. open-air   b. expensive   c. famous
2. traveling *incognito*
   a. cheaply   b. under an alias   c. quickly
3. a major *fiasco*
   a. cigar   b. fault   c. failure
4. an important *manifesto*
   a. declaration   b. expansion   c. bond issue
5. a real *dilettante*
   a. expert   b. socialite   c. amateur
6. a horrible *imbroglio*
   a. confusion   b. disgrace   c. conflagration
7. a broad *piazza*
   a. forest   b. error   c. town square
8. an expensive *replica*
   a. request   b. copy   c. machine
9. a famous *impresario*
   a. singer   b. actor   c. manager

Answers: 1. a   2. b   3. c   4. a   5. c
6. a   7. c   8. b   9. c

LESSON 4 🕐

ADDITIONAL ITALIAN BORROWINGS

Italian is often said to be the most musical of the Romance languages. Make sure to practice the pronunciations of the following musical and artistic terms borrowed from Italian. The two self-tests at the end of the lesson will help you reinforce the words and their meanings.

1. **sotto voce** (sot′ō vō′chē) in a low, soft voice, so as not to be overheard.
2. **sonata** (sə nä′tə) a composition for one or two instruments, typically with three or four contrasting movements.
3. **fugue** (fyo͞og) a polyphonic composition based on one, two, or more themes that are enunciated by several voices or parts in turn, and are subject to contrapuntal treatment; in psychiatry, a period in which a patient suffers from loss of memory, often begins a new life, and upon recovery, remembers nothing from the amnesiac period. Borrowed through French from Italian "fuga," literally *a fleeing, flight.*
4. **intermezzo** (in′tər met′sō, -med′zō) a short dramatic, musical, or other entertainment of light character introduced between the acts of a drama or opera.

5. **cantata** (kən tä′tə) a choral composition, either sacred and resembling a short oratorio, or secular, as a drama set to music but not to be acted.

6. **maestro** (mī′strō) an eminent composer, teacher, or conductor of music.

7. **chiaroscuro** (kē är′ə skyŏŏr′ō) the distribution of light and shade in a picture.

8. **villanella** (vil′ə nel′ə) a rustic Italian part-song without accompaniment. The French word "villanelle," meaning *a short poem of fixed form*, was adapted from Italian.

Test 1: Defining Words

Define each of the following words.

1. villanella _____
2. chiaroscuro _____
3. sonata _____
4. sotto voce _____
5. maestro _____
6. cantata _____
7. intermezzo _____
8. fugue _____

Suggested Answers: 1. a part-song without accompaniment 2. the distribution of light and shade in a picture 3. a musical composition for one or two instruments, typically with three or four

contrasting movements   4. in a low, soft voice
5. an eminent composer, teacher, or conductor of
music   6. a choral composition   7. a short, light
entertainment offered between the acts of a drama
or opera   8. a polyphonic composition based on
one or more themes

Test 2: True/False

In the space provided, write T if the definition of
the numbered word is true or F if it is false.

			T or F
1.	MAESTRO	famous musician	_____
2.	CHIAROSCURO	shadows	_____
3.	INTERMEZZO	musical interlude	_____
4.	CANTATA	song	_____
5.	SONATA	ballad	_____
6.	VILLANELLA	part-song	_____
7.	FUGUE	musical instrument	_____
8.	SOTTO VOCE	strident voice	_____

Answers: 1. T   2. T   3. T   4. F   5. F
6. T   7. F   8. F

LESSON 5 🕐

SPANISH BORROWINGS

Our neighbors to the south have also enriched
our language with a number of words that reflect
the merging of Spanish culture with our own.

You may find that you are already familiar with some of the following words but were unaware of their Hispanic ancestry.

1. **desperado** (des'pə rä'dō, -rä'-) a bold, reckless criminal or outlaw.
2. **fiesta** (fē es'tə) in Spain and Latin America, a festival celebrating a religious holiday; any festive celebration.
3. **siesta** (sē es'tə) a midday or afternoon rest or nap, especially as taken in Spain and Latin America.
4. **bonanza** (bə nan'zə, bō-) a rich mass of ore, as found in mining; a spectacular windfall.
5. **pronto** (pron'tō) promptly; quickly.
6. **patio** (pat'ē ō', pä'tē ō') a paved outdoor area adjoining a house; courtyard.
7. **bolero** (bə lâr'ō, bō-) a lively Spanish dance in triple meter; a waist-length jacket worn open in front.
8. **bravado** (brə vä'dō) swaggering display of courage.

Test 1: True/False

In the space provided, write T if the definition of the numbered word is true or F if it is false.

		T or F
1. SIESTA	nap	_____
2. PATIO	courtyard	_____

		T or F
3. BOLERO	jacket	_____
4. FIESTA	celebration	_____
5. BRAVADO	applause	_____
6. PRONTO	dappled pony	_____
7. DESPERADO	desperate lover	_____
8. BONANZA	sprawling ranch	_____

Answers: 1. T   2. T   3. T   4. T   5. F
6. F   7. F   8. F

Test 2: Matching Synonyms

Select the best definition for each numbered word. Write your answer in the space provided.

1. PRONTO	a. great, sudden wealth or luck	_____
2. BRAVADO	b. afternoon nap	_____
3. BONANZA	c. courtyard	_____
4. BOLERO	d. bold outlaw	_____
5. DESPERADO	e. festive celebration	_____
6. SIESTA	f. promptly	_____
7. PATIO	g. waist-length jacket	_____
8. FIESTA	h. swaggering show of bravery	_____

Answers: 1. f   2. h   3. a   4. g   5. d
6. b   7. c   8. e

LESSON 6 🕐

ADDITIONAL SPANISH BORROWINGS

Here are some additional Spanish words to spice up your speech and writing. Study the definitions and complete the two self-tests at the end of the lesson to help you reinforce what you have learned.

1. **tango** (tang′gō) a ballroom dance of Spanish-American origin.
2. **arroyo** (ə roi′ō) a small steep-sided watercourse or gulch with a nearly flat floor, usually dry except in heavy rains.
3. **sierra** (sē er′ə) a chain of hills or mountains, the peaks of which suggest the teeth of a saw.
4. **mesa** (mā′sə) a land formation having a flat top and steep rock walls, common in arid and semi-arid parts of the United States and Mexico.
5. **chili con carne** (chil′ē kon kär′nē) a spicy Mexican-American dish of meat, beans, onion, chopped pepper, tomatoes, and seasonings.
6. **guerrilla** (gə ril′ə) a member of a small, independent band of soldiers that harass the enemy by surprise raids, sabotage, etc.
7. **mustang** (mus′tang) a small, hardy horse of the American plains.

8. **caudillo** (kou thē′lyô, -thē′yô) a head of state, especially a military dictator.

Test 1: Definitions

For each definition, select the correct vocabulary word. Write your answer in the space provided.

_____ 1. a member of a band of independent soldiers who harass the enemy through surprise attacks
   a. quadroon   c. mustang
   b. arroyo   d. guerrilla

_____ 2. a Mexican-American dish of meat, beans, tomatoes, onion, chopped pepper, and seasonings
   a. sierra   c. chili con
   b. taco   carne
              d. peccadillo

_____ 3. a small, steep-sided watercourse or gulch with a nearly flat floor
   a. arroz con pollo   c. arroyo
   b. tango   d. mesa

_____ 4. a small, hardy horse
   a. arroyo   c. mesa
   b. mustang   d. caudillo

_____ 5. a military dictator
   a. caudillo   c. sierra
   b. mesa   d. arroyo

_____ 6. a ballroom dance of Spanish-American origin
   a. tango   c. quadroon
   b. waltz   d. arroyo

_____ 7. a land formation having a flat top
and steep rock walls
a. Sierra Madre   c. arroyo
b. tango   d. mesa
_____ 8. a chain of hills or mountains
a. quadroon   c. sierra
b. mesa   d. arroyo

Answers: 1. d   2. c   3. c   4. b   5. a
6. a   7. d   8. c

Test 2: Matching Synonyms

Match each of the numbered words with its closest synonym. Write your answer in the space provided.

1. MESA	a. soldier	_____
2. MUSTANG	b. saw-toothed mountains	_____
3. CAUDILLO	c. ballroom dance	_____
4. ARROYO	d. flat-topped land formation	_____
5. GUERRILLA	e. chief of state	_____
6. TANGO	f. spicy dish of meat and beans	_____
7. CHILI CON CARNE	g. dry gulch	_____
8. SIERRA	h. horse	_____

Answers: 1. d   2. h   3. e   4. g   5. a
6. c   7. f   8. b

LESSON 7 🕐

LATIN BORROWINGS

We've already encountered a great number of words with Latin roots in previous lessons, but most of them have been transformed over the centuries. Here are eight Latin words and phrases that survived intact when they were incorporated into English. All are words that can add power to your speech and writing. Study the definitions and complete the two self-tests.

1. **decorum** (di kôr′əm) dignified behavior, manners, or appearance.
2. **gratis** (grat′is, grā′tis) without charge or payment; free.
3. **in toto** (in tō′tō) in all; in the whole.
4. **odium** (ō′dē əm) intense hatred or dislike, especially toward something or someone regarded as contemptible, despicable, or repugnant.
5. **per se** (pûr sā′, sē′) by, of, for, or in itself.
6. **pro tempore** (prō′ tem′pə rē′, -rā′) temporarily; for the time being.
7. **status quo** (stā′təs kwō′, stat′əs) the existing state or condition; things as they are.
8. **terra firma** (ter′ə fûr′mə) firm or solid earth; dry land.

Test 1: Defining Words

Define each of the following words.

1. pro tempore _____
2. odium _____
3. in toto _____
4. per se _____
5. terra firma _____
6. decorum _____
7. gratis _____
8. status quo _____

Suggested Answers: 1. temporarily; for the time being 2. intense hatred or dislike 3. in all; in the whole 4. by, of, for, or in itself 5. firm or solid earth; dry land 6. dignified behavior, manners, or appearance 7. without charge or payment; free 8. the existing state or condition

Test 2: True/False

In the space provided, write T if the definition of the numbered word is true or F if it is false.

		T or F
1. STATUS QUO	existing state	_____
2. PRO TEMPORE	for the time being	_____
3. ODIUM	bad odor	_____
4. TERRA FIRMA	solid ground	_____
5. PER SE	amount	_____
6. IN TOTO	with the dog	_____
7. GRATIS	free	_____
8. DECORUM	embellishment	_____

Answers: 1. T 2. T 3. F 4. T 5. F 6. F 7. T 8. F

10. SPECIAL WORDS

LESSON 1 🕐

SLANG

Slang is a very informal use of vocabulary and idiom, typically formed by creative, often clever juxtapositions of images or words. It is characteristically more metaphorical, playful, elliptical, vivid, and ephemeral than ordinary language.

New slang expressions tend to come from subcultures, such as adolescents, ethnic minorities, citizen-band radio broadcasters, sports groups, criminals, and members of established institutions, such as the armed forces or labor unions. If members of the subculture have sufficient contact with the mainstream culture, the slang expression often passes into general use. For instance, "cool" (*fashionable, well-accepted*), "nitty-gritty" (*the core or crux of some matter*), and "The Man" (*the law*) all derive from the black culture of New York's Harlem area.

Slang develops just as other levels of language develop. In some instances, words acquire new meanings ("cat" for a *person*); in others, a meaning becomes extended ("fink," at first *a strikebreaker*, now refers to any betrayer). Words become abbreviated ("burger" for "hamburger," "perk" for "percolate"), and acronyms become widely used ("VIP"). Often words are created to deal with social and other innovations (as "tail-gating," "yuppie," "hip-hop").

Slang expressions can quickly become passé ("sheik," "skiddoo," "goo-goo eyes," "the cat's pajamas," "hepcat") or standard speech ("hand-me-down" for "second-hand item"). Today, mass communication has greatly speeded up the circulation of slang expressions.

While slang invigorates a language, giving it freshness and energy, it has no place in formal speech and writing. Use it occasionally to flavor your conversation, but be careful to suit your audience and purpose. Also, make sure the words you're using are not stale and out of date.

Test: Write In

Each of the following sentences contains an italicized slang word or expression that is perfectly appropriate in the context of informal conversation. For each sentence, replace the slang word with a word or phrase that would be better suited to more formal usage and notice the effect of the change. Write your answer in the space provided.

_____ 1. He really *bugs* me when he does that.

_____ 2. Slow down! *Smokey's* up ahead behind those bushes!

_____ 3. That chore was a real *pain in the neck*.

_____ 4. Johnny was hit on the *bean* with the softball.

_____ 5. I had a lot of *moola* riding on that bet.

_____ 6. I *blew* it all at the races.

_____ 7. That franchise deal was a *ripoff*.

_____ 8. If you keep on drinking like that, you're going to get *plastered*.

_____ 9. I wish he'd quit his *bellyaching*.

_____ 10. When she's in one of those moods, she's a real *sourpuss*.

_____ 11. He *zapped* the figures marching across the screen and defeated his opponent.

_____ 12. What's your *beef*?

_____ 13. I told him to *bug off*.

_____ 14. If he doesn't start studying soon, he's going to *flunk* this course.

_____ 15. Mike is *hooked on* video games.

Suggested Answers: 1. annoys, bothers 2. state highway trooper 3. nuisance, bother 4. head 5. money 6. spent, wasted 7. fraud, swindle 8. drunk 9. complaining, grumbling 10. complainer, grumbler, grouch 11. hit, destroyed,

demolished   12. complaint   13. leave, depart
14. fail   15. addicted to, obsessed with

LESSON 2 🕐

JARGON AND ARGOT

"Get him in here stat," the doctor ordered.
"Stat," a word adopted by the medical establishment from Latin "statim," is medical argot for
"immediately" and is used when doctors and
their assistants want to communicate quickly and
efficiently. Both "jargon" and "argot" refer to the
vocabulary that is peculiar to a specific group of
people and that has been devised for intergroup
communication or identification. Its use is also a
means of restricting access by the uninitiated
and creating a sense of exclusivity among group
members. Though the words "jargon" and "argot" are interchangeable, "jargon" has derogatory
tory connotations and one of its common
meanings is *gibberish, nonsense*. For that reason
we shall use the designation "argot" for spe-
cialized terminology.

While some argot does pass into general circulation, most of it remains incomprehensible to
the layperson. Argot should be used only within
the field to which it belongs; otherwise, it will
probably fail to communicate your meaning.
Here are some examples of argot drawn from
different disciplines.

LEGAL ARGOT

on all fours	a legal precedent exactly on the mark
blacklining	marking a legal document for changes
nit	a small point
conformed copy	a legal document with a printed rather than a signed name
counterparts	identical copies signed by different parties

PUBLISHING ARGOT

dummy	a mocked-up copy to be checked, as for pagination.
proof	a trial impression of composed type taken to correct errors and make alterations
gutter	the white space formed by the inner margins of two facing pages of a book
slush pile	unsolicited manuscripts

PRINTING ARGOT

bleed	illustration or printing that extends beyond the trim size of the page
roll size	paper width
live art	the actual art being used

blanket   the rubber sheet in a printing
                                    press that transfers the image
                                    from the plate to the paper

THEATER ARGOT

angel   a theatrical backer
spot   a spotlight
apron   the part of a stage in front of
                                    the curtain
ice   free tickets

COMPUTER ARGOT

boot up   to start a computer by loading
                                    the operating system
crash   a major computer malfunction
debug   to detect and correct errors in
                                    a system
interface   connection; interaction
on-line   connected to a main computer

AERONAUTICS ARGOT

jig   a device in which an airplane
                                    part can be held while it is be-
                                    ing worked on
BAFO   best and final offer
RFQ   request for quote
CDRL   contract data requirements list

Test: Matching Synonyms

Below are some examples of baseball argot. See
how closely you can match each word or phrase
with its meaning. Write your answer in the space
provided.

_____ 1. fungo

_____ 2. around the
horn

_____ 3. hit for the
cycle

_____ 4. can of corn

_____ 5. grand slam

_____ 6. Baltimore
chop

a. a high fly ball
that's easy to catch

b. batter hits the ball
down so it will
bounce high

c. a baseball tossed
in the air and
struck as it comes
down

d. a home run with
three runners on
base

e. to get a single,
double, triple, and
home run in one
game

f. a double play
started by the
third baseman

Answers: 1. c   2. f   3. e   4. a   5. d
6. b

LESSON 3 🕐

DIALECT AND BRITICISMS

A dialect is a version of language spoken in a particular geographic region or by a specific group of people. Dialects frequently contain words, pronunciations, and grammatical structures that are not accepted as standard English. For example, in the British Yorkshire dialect, "something" would be rendered as "summat."

Although the Americans and the British have little difficulty communicating with each other, each country nevertheless retains a vocabulary of its own. Words used specifically by the British are known as Briticisms. Here are some of the more common ones.

Americanism	Briticism
bar	pub
laid off (from a job)	redundant
raincoat	mackintosh
police officer, cop	bobby
guy	bloke
candy store	sweet-shop
crazy	barmy
druggist	chemist
TV	telly
gasoline	petrol
elevator	lift
run (in a stocking)	ladder
sofa	settee
subway	underground

Americanism	Briticism
hood (of a car)	bonnet
naked	starkers
napkin	serviette
truck	lorry
call up (on the telephone)	ring up
French-fried potatoes	chips

Test: Matching Synonyms

Match each Briticism with its American counterpart. Write your answer in the space provided

1.	lift	a.	napkin	_____
2.	underground	b.	sofa	_____
3.	telly	c.	hood (of a car)	_____
4.	barmy	d.	truck	_____
5.	chips	e.	guy	_____
6.	redundant	f.	elevator	_____
7.	settee	g.	druggist	_____
8.	petrol	h.	TV	_____
9.	bloke	i.	police officer, cop	_____
10.	bobby	j.	run (in a stocking)	_____
11.	lorry	k.	subway	_____
12.	chemist	l.	crazy	_____
13.	ring up	m.	call up	_____
14.	mackintosh	n.	gasoline	_____
15.	serviette	o.	raincoat	_____
16.	pub	p.	French fries	_____
17.	sweet-shop	q.	bar	_____
18.	ladder	r.	laid off	_____
19.	bonnet	s.	candy store	_____
20.	starkers	t.	naked	_____

11. PUZZLES

It's no surprise that people who love to solve word puzzles have superior vocabularies. Here are a number of different puzzles designed to add to *your* word power. There are three different types of puzzles to tease your brain and augment your vocabulary. Have fun!

LESSON 1 🕐

SUPER SIX

Most of the words in this puzzle have six letters; two of them have five. Your job is to fit each word listed below in its proper place in the puzzle. To help you get started, we've filled in one word, "mantra."

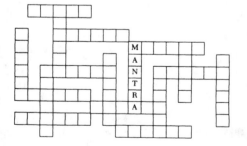

Word List

1. **cabal** (kə bal') a small group of conspirators, especially one plotting against a government
2. **fecund** (fē'kund, fek'und) prolific, fertile, fruitful
3. **bisque** (bisk) a heavy cream soup of puréed shellfish or vegetables; ice cream made with powdered macaroons or nuts
4. **drivel** (driv'əl) nonsense
5. **bungle** (bung'gəl) to do clumsily or awkwardly; botch
6. **wimple** (wim'pəl) a woman's headcloth drawn in folds under the chin, formerly worn out of doors, and still in use by nuns
7. **morose** (mə rōs') gloomy, depressed
8. **balsam** (bôl'səm) a fragrant resin exuded from certain trees
9. **demean** (di mēn') to lower in dignity or standing; debase
10. **petard** (pi tärd') an engine of war or an explosive device formerly used to blow in a door or gate, form a breach in a wall, etc.
11. **mantra** (man'trə, män'-) a word or formula to be recited or sung
12. **feisty** (fī'stē) animated, energetic, spirited, plucky
13. **welter** (wel'tər) to roll, toss, or heave, as waves; to wallow or become deeply involved
14. **supine** (sōō pīn') lying on the back

15. **beadle** (bēd'l) in British universities, an official who supervises and leads processions; macebearer; a parish officer who keeps order during services, waits on the clergy, etc.

16. **duress** (dŏŏ res', dyŏŏ-) coercion, force, constraint

17. **sinew** (sin'yŏŏ) tendon; a source of strength

Answers:

```
      C A B A L
        I
  F     S U P I N E
  E     Q           M O R O S E
  C     U       D   A       I     F
  U   W E L T E R   N B U N G L E
  N   I         I   E   E   E   I
  D E M E A N   V   R   A   W   S
      P       P E T A R D       T
  B A L S A M L     D   L       Y
      E           D U R E S S
```

LESSON 2 🕐

WORD FIND #1

There are seventeen words hidden in this word find puzzle. To complete the puzzle, locate and circle all the words. The words may be written forward, backward, up, or down. Good luck!

```
C A T A F A L Q U E D
R D N U C I B U R T E
U E P O I L L A C A T
C S C A R A B G D G A
I O Z O B E R M I E C
B E L B U A B I C N I
L E Z A R A S R U B T
E F O N T A N E L A S
B S A T U R N A L I A
M S I P O R P A L A M
```

Word List:

1. **malapropism** (mal'ə prop iz'əm) the act or habit of misusing words ridiculously
2. **rubicund** (rōō'bi kund') red or reddish
3. **saturnalia** (sat'ər nā'lē ə) unrestrained revelry; orgy
4. **catafalque** (kat'ə fôk', -fôlk', -falk') a raised structure on which the body of a deceased person lies in state
5. **quagmire** (kwag'mīr', kwog'-) an area of miry or boggy ground
6. **lucid** (lōō'sid) crystal-clear
7. **bauble** (bô'bəl) a cheap piece of ornamentation; gewgaw
8. **masticated** (mas'ti kā'tid) chewed
9. **calliope** (kə lī'ə pē') a musical instrument consisting of a set of harsh-sounding steam whistles that are activated by a keyboard

10. **rebozo** (ri bō'sō, -zō) a long woven scarf, worn over the head and shoulders, especially by Mexican women

11. **rubric** (rōō'brik) a title, heading, direction, or the like, in a book, written or printed in red or otherwise distinguished from the rest of the text

12. **fontanel** (fon'tn el') one of the spaces, covered by a membrane, between the bones of the fetal or young skull

13. **raze** (rāz) to wreck, demolish

14. **scarab** (skar'əb) a beetle regarded as sacred by the ancient Egyptians; a representation or image of a beetle, much used by the ancient Egyptians

15. **abnegate** (ab'ni gāt') to surrender or renounce (rights, conveniences, etc.); deny oneself

16. **bursar** (bûr'sər, -sär) a treasurer or business officer, especially of a college or university

17. **crucible** (krōō'sə bəl) a vessel of metal or refractory material employed for heating substances to a high temperature

Answers:

```
C A T A F A L Q U E D
R D N U C I B U R T   E
U E P O I L L A C   A T
C S C A R A B G D G A C
I O Z O B E R M I C   I
B E L B U A B I C   E T
L E Z A R A S R U B   S
E F O N T A N E L A   A
B S A T U R N A L I A A
M S I P O R P A L A   M
```

ACROSTIC #1

First unscramble each of the seven vocabulary words so that it matches its definition. Then use the words to fill in the appropriate spaces on the correspondingly numbered lines. When you have completed the entire puzzle, another vocabulary word will read vertically in the first spaces.

1. PONILANER having no equal
2. YOGLUE a speech or writing in praise of a person
3. MERRYPUT nonsense
4. REESIO an evening party or social gathering
5. HUNRIC a mischievous child
6. SIKKO an open pavilion
7. TEARRA errors in writing or printing

1. __ __ __ __ __ __ __ __ __
2. __ __ __ __ __ __
3. __ __ __ __ __ __ __ __
4. __ __ __ __ __ __
5. __ __ __ __ __ __
6. __ __ __ __ __
7. __ __ __ __ __ __

Word List:

soirée   errata   nonpareil
eulogy   trumpery   kiosk   urchin

Answers:

<u>n o n p a r e i l</u> having no equal

<u>e u l o g y</u> a speech or writing in praise of a person

<u>t r u m p e r y</u> nonsense

<u>s o i r é e</u> an evening party or social gathering

<u>u r c h i n</u> a mischievous child

<u>k i o s k</u> an open pavilion

<u>e r r a t a</u> errors in writing or printing

(**netsuke** (net′skē, -skä) in Japanese art, a small carved figure, originally used as a buttonlike fixture on a man's sash)

LESSON 4 🕐

WORD FIND #2

There are eighteen words hidden in this word find puzzle. To complete the puzzle, locate and circle all the words. The words may be written forward, backward, up, or down. Good luck!

```
N O N S E Q U I T U R
E B G A D F L Y B O E
T A U T O L O G Y E M
T L D U E U R O D N O
L U A R P U R L O I N
E S M N A C L O Y T S
S T S I J S U X E N T
O R O N E C N O N O R
M A N E M L O D B T A
E D S O D E N R U O T
P E J O R A T I V E E
```

Word List:

1. **nonce** (nons) the present; the immediate occasion or purpose
2. **damson** (dam′zən, -sən) the small dark-blue or purple fruit of a plum
3. **nexus** (nek′səs) a means of connecting; tie; link
4. **jape** (jāp) to jest; joke; jibe
5. **tontine** (ton′tēn, ton tēn′) an annuity scheme in which subscribers share a common fund with the benefit of survivorship, the survivors' shares being increased as the subscribers die, until the whole goes to the last survivor
6. **balustrade** (bal′ə strād′, bal′ə strād′) a railing
7. **doxology** (dok sol′ə jē) a hymn or form of words containing an ascription of praise to God
8. **non sequitur** (non sek′wi tər, -tōōr′) an inference or conclusion that does not follow from the premises
9. **purloin** (pər loin′, pûr′loin) to take dishonestly; steal
10. **dolmen** (dōl′men, -mən, dol′-) a structure, usually regarded as a tomb, consisting of two or more large, upright stones set with a space between and capped by a horizontal stone
11. **doyen** (doi en′, doi′ən) the senior member, as in age or rank, of a group

12. **remonstrate** (ri mon′strāt) to protest
13. **nettlesome** (net′l səm) annoying; disturbing
14. **tautology** (tô tol′ə jē) needless repetition of an idea in different words, as in "widow woman"
15. **rue** (rōō) to deplore; mourn; regret
16. **gadfly** (gad′flī′) a person who repeatedly and persistently annoys or stirs up others with provocative criticism
17. **pejorative** (pə jôr′ə tiv, -jor′-) having a disparaging, derogatory, or belittling effect or force
18. **saturnine** (sat′ər nīn′) having or showing a sluggish, gloomy temperament

Answers:

N	O	N	S	E	Q	U	I	T	U	R
E	B	G	A	D	F	L	Y	B	O	E
T	A	U	T	O	L	O	G	Y	E	M
T	L	D	U	E	U	R	O	D	N	O
L	U	A	R	P	U	R	L	O	I	N
E	S	M	N	A	C	L	O	Y	T	S
S	T	S	I	J	S	U	X	E	N	T
O	R	O	N	E	C	N	O	N	O	R
M	A	N	E	M	L	O	D	B	T	A
E	D	S	O	D	E	N	R	U	O	T
P	E	J	O	R	A	T	I	V	E	E

LESSON 5 🕐

ACROSTIC #2

First unscramble each of the seven vocabulary
words so that it matches its definition. Then use
the words to fill in the appropriate spaces on the
correspondingly numbered lines. When you have
completed the entire puzzle, another vocabulary
word will read vertically in the first spaces.

1. RACEUSA a break, usually in the middle of a
   verse
2. ORAMIRE a large wardrobe
3. BAMNELT moving lightly over a surface
4. SOURIOUX doting upon or submissive to
   one's wife
5. CANDIMENT a beggar
6. MYPONE a person, real or imaginary, from
   whom something, as a tribe, nation, or place,
   takes its name
7. FITFIN a light lunch (British usage)

1. __ __ __ __ __ __ __
2. __ __ __ __ __ __ __
3. __ __ __ __ __ __ __
4. __ __ __ __ __ __ __ __
5. __ __ __ __ __ __ __ __ __
6. __ __ __ __ __ __
7. __ __ __ __ __ __

Word List:

tiffin lambent mendicant

eponym caesura armoire uxorious

Answers:

c a e s u r a a break, usually in the middle of a verse

a r m o i r e a large wardrobe

l a m b e n t moving lightly over a surface

u x o r i o u s doting upon or submissive to one's wife

m e n d i c a n t a beggar

e p o n y m a person, real or imaginary, from whom something, as a tribe, nation, or place, takes its name

t i f f i n a light lunch (British usage)

(**calumet** (kal'yə met', kal'yə met') a long, ornamented ceremonial tobacco pipe used by Native Americans)

LESSON 6 🕐

WORD FIND #3

There are fourteen words hidden in this word find puzzle. To complete the puzzle, locate and circle all the words. The words may be written forward, backward, up, or down. Good luck!

```
D  N  U  B  R  E  M  M  U  C
U  N  A  M  S  D  U  B  M  O
L  C  O  B  E  Z  A  G  A  M
C  O  A  L  E  S  C  E  H  P
I  I  M  Y  R  I  A  D  O  O
M  F  E  Y  N  E  E  R  U  T
E  T  I  O  L  O  G  Y  T  E
R  O  U  S  T  A  B  O  U  T
```

Word List:

1. **gazebo** (gə zā′bō, -zē′-) a structure, as a summerhouse or pavilion, built on a site affording a pleasant view
2. **roustabout** (roust′ə bout′) a wharf laborer or deck hand; a circus laborer
3. **compote** (kom′pōt) fruit stewed or cooked in syrup
4. **coif** (kwäf, koif) a hairstyle
5. **cummerbund** (kum′ər bund′) a wide sash worn as a waistband, especially one with horizontal pleats worn beneath a dinner jacket
6. **seer** (sēr) a prophet; mystic
7. **ombudsman** (om′bədz mən, -man′, -bŏŏdz-, ôm′-) a commissioner appointed by a legislature to hear and investigate complaints by private citizens against government officials and agencies
8. **mahout** (mə hout′) the keeper or driver of an elephant

9. **tureen** (tŏō rēn', tyŏō-) a large, deep covered dish for serving soup or stew
10. **coalesce** (kō'ə les') to blend; join
11. **fey** (fā) fairylike; whimsical or strange; su-
    pernatural, enchanted; in unnaturally high
    spirits
12. **etiology** (ē'tē ol'ə jē) the study of the
    causes of diseases
13. **dulcimer** (dul'sə mər) a trapezoidal
    zither with metal strings that are struck with
    light hammers
14. **myriad** (mir'ē əd) many; innumerable

Answers:

```
D N U B R E M M U C
U N A M S D U B M O
L C O B E Z A G A M
C O A L E S C E H P
I I M Y R I A D O O
M F E Y N E E R U T
E T I O L O G Y T E
R O U S T A B O U T
```

LESSON 7 🕐

THE "P" PATCH

Each of the words in this puzzle begins with the
letter "p." Your job is to fit each of the words
listed below in its proper place in the puzzle. To
help you get started, we've filled in one word,
"pimpernel."

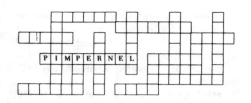

Word List:

1. **patois** (pat′wä, pä′twä, pa twä′) a rural or provincial form of speech, especially of French

2. **parse** (pärs, pärz) to describe (a word or series of words) grammatically, telling the parts of speech, inflectional forms, etc.

3. **poteen** (pə tēn′, -chēn′) illicitly distilled whiskey

4. **pimpernel** (pim′pər nel′, -nl) a plant of the primrose family, having scarlet, purplish, or white flowers that close at the approach of bad weather

5. **piebald** (pī′bôld′) having patches of black and white or of other colors

6. **paean** (pē′ən) any song of praise, joy, or thanksgiving

7. **prosody** (pros′ə dē) the science or study of poetic meters and versification

8. **pica** (pī′kə) a type size measuring twelve points

9. **pout** (pout) to sulk; look sullen

10. **pastiche** (pa stēsh', pä-) a literary, musical, or artistic piece consisting wholly or chiefly of motifs or techniques borrowed from one or more sources

11. **pariah** (pə rī'ə) an outcast

12. **piddle** (pid'l) to waste time; dawdle

13. **placebo** (plə sē'bō) a substance having no pharmacological effect but given to a patient or subject of an experiment who supposes it to be a medicine

14. **paucity** (pô'si tē) scarcity; meagerness or scantiness

15. **peon** (pē'ən, -on) an unskilled laborer; drudge; person of low social status

16. **pupa** (pyōō'pə) an insect in the nonfeeding, usually immobile, transformation stage between the larva and the imago

17. **pinto** (pin'tō, pēn'-) piebald; mottled; spotted; a pinto horse

Answers:

LESSON 8 🕐

WORD FIND #4

There are twenty words hidden in this word find puzzle. To complete the puzzle, locate and circle all the words. The words may be written forward, backward, up, or down. Good luck!

```
T  S  I  T  A  M  S  I  M  U  N  B
C  A  C  H  E  P  O  T  U  O  L  F
A  P  F  E  R  A  L  R  S  E  E  R
L  X  R  A  M  S  A  I  M  R  N  E
L  U  D  D  I  T  E  A  O  T  G  N
O  A  Z  Y  A  I  K  G  I  U  I  E
U  F  A  D  O  C  H  E  R  O  O  T
S  S  C  A  T  H  A  R  S  I  S  I
C  A  S  E  M  E  N  T  Y  O  L  C
```

Word List:

1. **triage** (trē äzh′) the process of sorting victims, as of a battle or disaster, to determine priority of medical treatment
2. **cachepot** (kash′pot′, -pō′) an ornamental container for holding or concealing a flowerpot
3. **frenetic** (frə net′ik) highly excited
4. **callous** (kal′əs) unfeeling
5. **miasma** (mī az′mə, mē-) noxious exhalations from putrescent matter

6. **outré** (o͞o trā′) beyond the bounds of what is usual or considered proper

7. **cheroot** (shə ro͞ot′) a cigar having open, untapered ends

8. **feral** (fēr′əl, fer′-) wild, primitive

9. **flout** (flout) to treat with disdain, scorn, or contempt; scoff at

10. **catharsis** (kə thär′sis) purging of the emotions, especially through a work of art

11. **Luddite** (lud′īt) a member of any of various bands of English workers (1811–1816) who destroyed industrial machinery in the belief that its use diminished employment; any opponent of new technologies

12. **faux pas** (fō pä′) a social gaffe; error

13. **soigné** (swän yā′) carefully or elegantly done; well-groomed

14. **seer** (sēr) a prophet; mystic

15. **numismatist** (no͞o miz′mə tist, -mis′-, nyo͞o-) a person who collects coins

16. **pastiche** (pa stēsh′, pä-) a literary, musical, or artistic piece consisting wholly or chiefly of motifs or techniques borrowed from one or more sources

17. **heady** (hed′ē) intoxicating; exciting

18. **coda** (kō′də) a passage concluding a musical composition

19. **cloy** (kloi) to weary by excess, as of food, sweetness, or pleasure; surfeit or sate

20. **casement** (kās′mənt) a window sash opening on hinges

```
T  S  I  T  A  M  S  I  M  U  N  B
C  A  C  H  E  P  O  T  U  O  L  F
A  P  F  E  R  A  L  R  S  E  E  R
L  X  R  A  M  S  A  I  M  R  N  E
L  U  D  D  I  T  E  A  O  T  G  N
O  A  Z  Y  A  I  K  G  I  U  I  E
U  F  A  D  O  C  H  E  R  O  O  T
S  S  C  A  T  H  A  R  S  I  S  I
C  A  S  E  M  E  N  T  Y  O  L  C
```

LESSON 9 🕐

ACROSTIC #3

First unscramble each of the seven vocabulary
words so that it matches its definition. Then use
the words to fill in the appropriate spaces on the
correspondingly numbered lines. When you have
completed the entire puzzle, another vocabulary
word will read vertically in the first spaces.

1. ZIMZUNE a crier who calls Muslims to
   prayer
2. NEXUPGE to erase
3. DAILYRAP the art of cutting and polishing
   gems; highly exact and refined in style
4. PARTIFIE a small alcoholic drink taken before dinner
5. COCARMENNY black magic; conjuration
6. TIGMEL a small tool; a cocktail
7. WESHEC to shun; avoid

1. __ __ __ __ __ __ __
2. __ __ __ __ __ __ __
3. __ __ __ __ __ __ __
4. __ __ __ __ __ __ __ __
5. __ __ __ __ __ __ __ __ __
6. __ __ __ __ __ __
7. __ __ __ __ __ __

Word List:

eschew   necromancy   lapidary
   gimlet   muezzin   apéritif   expunge

Answers:

m u e z z i n   a crier who calls Muslims to prayer
e x p u n g e   to erase
l a p i d a r y   the art of cutting and polishing gems;
highly exact and refined in style
a p é r i t i f   a small alcoholic drink taken before
dinner
n e c r o m a n c y   black magic; conjuration
g i m l e t   a small tool; a cocktail
e s c h e w   to shun; avoid

(**mélange** (mā läNzh', -länj') a mixture or
medley)

WORD FIND #5

There are thirteen words hidden in this word find puzzle. To complete the puzzle, locate and circle all the words. The words may be written forward, backward, up, or down. Good luck!

```
S  L  U  M  G  U  L  L  I  O  N  S  M
C  I  T  C  E  L  C  E  N  B  O  R  I
A  N  E  D  E  M  A  N  A  V  R  I  N
B  A  H  E  G  E  M  O  N  Y  O  X  A
R  E  C  A  N  T  E  D  E  R  M  I  R
O  A  A  E  P  I  P  H  A  N  Y  L  E
U  P  C  E  T  A  U  N  E  T  X  E  T
S  A  N  C  T  I  M  O  N  I  O  U  S
```

Word List:

1. **slumgullion** (slum gul′yən, slum′gul′-) a stew of meat, potatoes, and vegetables
2. **oxymoron** (ok′si môr′on) a figure of speech in which a locution produces an effect by seeming self-contradictory, as in "cruel kindness" or "to make haste slowly"
3. **paean** (pē′ən) any song of praise, joy, or thanksgiving
4. **minarets** (min′ə rets′, min′ə rets′) slender towers or turrets that are attached to a mosque and from which a muezzin calls the people to prayer

5. **sanctimonious** (sangk'tə mō'nē əs) insincere, hypocritical
6. **hegemony** (hi jem'ə nē, hej'ə mō'nē) leadership or predominant influence
7. **inane** (i nān') pointless, silly
8. **extenuate** (ik sten'yōō āt') to make or try to make seem less serious, especially by offering excuses
9. **nirvana** (nir vä'nə, -van'ə, nər-) in Buddhism, freedom from the endless cycle of personal reincarnations, with their consequent suffering, as a result of the extinction of individual passion, hatred, and delusion
10. **recanted** (ri kan'tid) retracted; denied
11. **edema** (i dē'mə) abnormal accumulation of fluids in body tissues, causing swelling
12. **epiphany** (i pif'ə nē) an appearance or manifestation, especially of a deity
13. **eclectic** (i klek'tik) selecting; choosing from various sources

Answers:

```
S L U M G U L L I O N S M
C I T C E L C E N B O R I
A N E D E M A N A V R I N
B A A H E G E M O N Y O X A
R E C A N T E D E R M I R
O A A E P I P H A N Y L E
U P C E T A U N E T X E T
S A N C T I M O N I O U S
```

LESSON 11 🕐

SPECTACULAR SEVEN

Each of the words in this puzzle has seven letters. Your job is to fit each of the words listed below in its proper place in the puzzle. To help you get started, we've filled in one word, "heinous," which means *reprehensible* or *evil*.

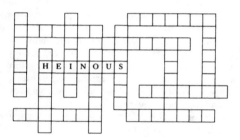

Word List:

1. **acolyte** (ak'ə līt') an altar boy
2. **pismire** (pis'mīᵊr', piz'-) an ant
3. **shoguns** (shō'gənz, -gunz) the chief Japanese military commanders from the eighth to twelfth centuries, or the hereditary officials who governed Japan, with the emperor as nominal ruler, until 1868
4. **panacea** (pan'ə sē'ə) a remedy for all ills; cure-all

5. **pooh-bah** (pōō'bä') a person who holds several positions, especially ones that give him importance; a pompous person
6. **hirsute** (hûr'sōōt, hûr sōōt') hairy
7. **foibles** (foi'bəlz) minor weaknesses or failings of character
8. **debacle** (də bä'kəl, -bak'əl, dā-) a general breakup or dispersion; sudden collapse
9. **carping** (kär'ping) fault-finding; critical
10. **cuckold** (kuk'əld) the husband of an unfaithful wife
11. **distaff** (dis'taf) a staff with a cleft end for holding wool, flax, etc., from which the thread is drawn in spinning by hand; the female sex; woman's work
12. **palfrey** (pôl'frē) a riding horse, as distinguished from a war horse; a woman's horse
13. **winsome** (win'səm) cute, charming

Answers:

A			P					C	U	C	K	O	L	D
C	A	R	P	I	N	G		H						E
O			S			D	I	S	T	A	F	F		B
L		S		M		P		R			O			A
Y		H	E	I	N	O	U	S			I			C
T		O		R		O		U			B			L
E		G		E		H		T		P	A	L	F	R	E	Y
		U				B		E			E			
P	A	N	A	C	E	A			W	I	N	S	O	M	E
		S				H								

LESSON 12 🕐

WORD FIND #6

There are nineteen words hidden in this word find puzzle. To complete the puzzle, locate and circle all the words. The words may be written forward, backward, up, or down. Good luck!

```
P  R  E  L  A  P  S  A  R  I  A  N
E  E  M  E  T  I  E  R  V  U  E  O
I  M  B  R  O  G  L  I  O  B  H  I
G  O  D  H  A  R  M  A  O  G  C  T
N  T  E  S  P  O  U  S  E  H  U  A
O  I  B  T  I  B  M  A  G  E  A  R
I  P  A  N  D  E  M  I  C  R  G  O
R  E  C  A  F  F  E  F  A  K  I  R
R  S  A  V  O  I  R  F  A  I  R  E
T  N  A  C  I  R  Y  G  E  N  A  P
```

Word List:

1. **peroration** (per'ə rā'shən) the concluding part of a speech or discourse

2. **oeuvre** (ûrv, ûrv'rə) the works of a writer, painter, or the like, taken as a whole

3. **prelapsarian** (prē'lap sâr'ē ən) pertaining to conditions existing before the fall of humankind

4. **mummery** (mum'ə rē) an empty or ostentatious performance

5. **gherkin** (gûr′kin) a pickle
6. **fakir** (fə kēr′, fā′kər) a Muslim or Hindu religious ascetic or mendicant monk commonly considered a wonder worker
7. **métier** (mā′tyā, mā tyā′) an occupation
8. **peignoir** (pān wär′, pen-, pān′wär, pen′-) a woman's dressing gown
9. **pandemic** (pan dem′ik) (of a disease) prevalent throughout an entire country or continent or the whole world
10. **savoir faire** (sav′wär fâr′) a knowledge of just what to do in any situation; tact
11. **gauche** (gōsh) uncouth; awkward
12. **imbroglio** (im brōl′yō) a confused state of affairs
13. **panegyric** (pan′i jir′ik, -jī′rik) an oration, discourse, or writing in praise of a person or thing
14. **dharma** (där′mə, dur′-) in Buddhism, the essential quality or nature, as of the cosmos or one's own character
15. **efface** (i fās′) to wipe out; cancel or obliterate; make (oneself) inconspicuous
16. **espouse** (i spouz′, i spous′) to advocate or support; marry
17. **epitome** (i pit′ə mē) a person or thing that is typical of or possesses to a high degree the features of a whole class; embodiment
18. **gambit** (gam′bit) in chess, an opening in which a player seeks by sacrificing a pawn or piece to obtain some advantage; any maneuver by which one seeks to gain an advantage

19. **cant** (kant) deceit; insincerity or hypoc-
    risy; the private language of a group, class, or
    profession; singsong or whining speech

Answers:

```
P R E L A P S A R I A N
E E M E T I E R V U E O
I M B R O G L I O B H I
G O D H A R M A O G C T A
N T E S P O U S E H U R
O I B T I B M A G E A O
I P A N D E M I C R G R
R E C A F F E F A K I R
R S A V O I R F A I R E
T N A C I R Y G E N A P
```

INDEX OF
VOCABULARY WORDS

abdication, 77, 79, 80
abduct, 81, 83
aberration, 161, 164, 165
ablution, 108, 109, 110
abnegate, 298
abominate, 161, 164, 165
abracadabra, 162, 164, 165
abreast, 32
abrupt, 45
abstemious, 36
abyss, 31
accelerometer, 48
accord, 27
accredited, 26
acolyte, 316
adhere, 46
adieu, 168, 170, 171
adjudicate, 26
advent, 46
advocate, 150, 152
aegis, 167, 169, 171
affidavit, 89, 90
agent, 46
agile, 6
agnostic, 31
alfresco, 271, 272, 273
alias, 50, 52

alien, 50, 52
alienate, 51, 52, 53
allegory, 50, 52, 53
allogamy, 51, 52, 53
allograft, 51, 52, 53
alluvium, 108, 109, 110
alma mater, 122, 124
aloof, 168, 169, 171
alopecia, 20
alter ego, 51, 52, 53
altercation, 51, 52, 53
altruism, 51, 52, 53
amazon, 171, 174, 175
amblyopia, 14
ambrosia, 165, 170, 171
ameliorate, 10
amenable, 37
anarchy, 68, 71, 72
anemone, 171, 175
anesthetic, 30
angelic, 39
Anglophile, 141, 143
Anglophobia, 49
anima, 53
animadversion, 54, 56
animalcule, 55, 56, 57
animate, 55, 56, 57
animation, 54, 56, 57

animism, 55, 56, 57
animus, 54, 56
anniversary, 58, 60, 61
annual, 58, 60, 61
annuity, 59, 60, 61
anonymous, 7, 30, 49
anthropocentric, 63, 64
anthropoid, 62, 63, 64
anthropology, 62, 63, 64
anthropomorphism, 62, 63, 64
antimacassar, 242, 243, 239
apartheid, 233, 237, 238
apathy, 48
apéritif, 313
apocryphal, 14, 31
apogee, 29, 31
apostasy, 29
apostle, 30
apotheosis, 148, 149
append, 144, 145, 146
appendage, 144, 145, 146
appendicitis, 41
apropos, 19
aquiline, 10
Arcadian, 224, 227, 228
archaic, 70, 72
archbishop, 69, 70, 72
archenemy, 68, 71, 72
archetype, 70, 71
argosy, 225, 227, 228
armoire, 305
arroyo, 279, 281
artifact, 85, 87

ascribe, 26
aseptic, 29
assiduity, 36
aster, 47
asteroid, 48
astro, 47
atavism, 37
audacious, 6
auriferous, 40
avant-garde, 264, 265, 266
avocation, 150, 152
badinage, 14
baffling, 6
bailiwick, 16
balkanize, 227, 228
ballyhoo, 228, 232, 233
balsam, 295
balustrade, 302
baroque, 16
bauble, 297
beadle, 296
bedaub, 32
begrudge, 33
beguile, 33
belfry, 177, 180, 181
bemoan, 32
bemuse, 33
benediction, 77, 79, 80
beseech, 32
bestowed, 32
bibliophile, 140, 143
bicentennial, 59, 60, 61
biennial, 58, 60, 61
billingsgate, 232, 233

biodegradable, 72, 76
bioengineering, 72, 76
biofeedback, 72, 76
biohazard, 72, 76
biological clock, 72, 76
bionic, 72, 76
biopsy, 72, 76
biota, 72, 76
biped, 133, 134, 136
bisque, 295
blarney, 253, 256, 258
blasé, 16
blitzkrieg, 259, 262
bluestocking, 168, 170,
  171
bohemian, 255, 256, 257
bolero, 277, 278
bolshevik, 245, 247, 248
bon vivant, 265, 266
bona fide, 88, 89, 90
bonanza, 277, 278
bootlegger, 156, 160
bowdlerize, 158, 160
boycott, 158, 160
bravado, 277, 278
bromide, 234, 237
bugbear, 156, 160, 161
bungle, 295
bursar, 298
cabal, 295
cabochon, 17
cabriolet, 17
cache, 17
cachepot, 310
cacophony, 48

cadaver, 46
caesura, 305
cajole, 9
calliope, 297
callous, 310
canard, 22
candor, 10
cant, 320
cantata, 275, 276
caprice, 231, 232, 233
captive, 44
carditis, 40
careless, 39
carnage, 40
carping, 317
casement, 311
castigate, 38
catafalque, 297
catharsis, 311
catholic, 10
caudillo, 280, 281
cause célèbre, 264, 265,
  266
caustic, 8
cavalier, 8
caveat, 8
cavil, 19
centennial, 59, 60, 61
chagrin, 236, 237, 238
chassis, 21
chauffeur, 267, 268, 270
chauvinism, 159, 160,
  161
cheroot, 311
chiaroscuro, 275, 276

chic, 268, 269
chicanery, 20
chili con carne, 279, 281
chiropodist, 133, 135
chromatic, 48
chromatics, 48
circumambulate, 23
circumference, 23
circumfluent, 23
circumfuse, 23
circumjacent, 23
circumlocution, 23
circumlunar, 23
circumnavigate, 23
circumpolar, 23
circumrotate, 23
circumscribe, 23
claustrophobia, 48
cloy, 311
coalesce, 307
coda, 311
cognition, 49, 66, 67
cognizant, 65, 67
cognoscenti, 66, 67
cohabit, 27
coif, 306
collateral, 26
collegiate, 36
colloquial, 111, 112
combustible, 36
compendium, 144, 145, 146
complacent, 136, 138, 139
complaisant, 137, 138

compote, 306
compress, 26
concurrent, 46
confederation, 26
confide, 88, 89, 90
confluence, 91, 92, 93
congenial, 95, 97
congenital, 94, 97
congress, 99, 101
conical, 40
connoisseur, 267, 268, 271
contumacious, 21
convoke, 150, 152
convolution, 27
copperhead, 230, 232, 233
cornucopia, 172, 175
cosmography, 49
cosmopolitan, 48
cosmos, 48
coup d'état, 263, 265, 266
covert, 10
craftsmanship, 41
cravat, 226, 227, 228
crucible, 298
cuckold, 317
cul-de-sac, 264, 265, 266
culpable, 37
cummerbund, 306
cupidity, 16
curvaceous, 39
cynosure, 176, 181, 182
dacha, 14
damson, 302

debacle, 317
debauch, 177, 181
debauched, 181
decennial, 58, 60, 61
décolletage, 267, 268, 269
decorum, 282, 283
deduce, 81, 83
defalcation, 21
degrade, 99, 101
dehydrate, 103, 107
deleterious, 37
demean, 295
democracy, 49
demographics, 49
denouement, 19
desperado, 277, 278
desultory, 167, 169, 171
dharma, 319
diadem, 172, 174, 175
diagnostician, 65, 67
dictum, 79, 80
digress, 99, 101
dilettante, 271, 272, 273
dilute, 108, 109, 110
diluvial, 108, 109, 110
dishabille, 14
disheveled, 6
dissection, 45
distaff, 317
diva, 21
dolmen, 302
doxology, 302
doyen, 302
drivel, 295

ductile, 82, 83
dulcimer, 307
duress, 296
dybbuk, 18
ebullient, 163, 164, 165
eclectic, 315
edema, 315
edict, 77, 79, 80
efface, 319
effeminacy, 14
effusive, 14
élan, 14
eldorado, 178, 181, 182
elision, 19
elocution, 112
eloquent, 111, 112
elucidate, 115, 116
emollient, 21
enclave, 163, 164, 165
engender, 94, 97
ennui, 22
entrepreneur, 259, 262
envoy, 263, 265, 266
epicure, 173, 175
epidemic, 48
epidermis, 30
epigram, 29
epiphany, 315
episode, 29
epithet, 30
epitome, 319
eponym, 305
equivocal, 151, 152
errata, 301
erudite, 11

eschew, 10, 313
escutcheon, 17
esoteric, 173, 175
espouse, 319
esprit de corps, 264, 265, 266
esquire, 178, 181, 182
etiology, 307
eugenics, 94, 97
eulogy, 301
eunuch, 254, 256, 257
evoke, 150, 152
evolve, 46
ewer, 21
excommunicate, 27
exegesis, 14
exigency, 10
expatriate, 128, 132
expedient, 133, 134, 135
expedite, 163, 165
expunge, 163, 164, 165, 313
extenuate, 315
facade, 20
facile, 85, 87
facsimile, 85, 87
factious, 84, 87
factitious, 85, 87
factotum, 84, 87
fakir, 319
faux pas, 311
fealty, 38
febrile, 15
fecund, 295
feign, 6, 9

feisty, 295
fellowship, 40
feral, 311
fey, 307
fiancé, 268, 270
fiasco, 156, 160, 271, 272, 273
fiat, 21
fidelity, 88, 89, 90
fiduciary, 88, 89, 90
fiesta, 277, 278
filibuster, 178, 181, 182
flaccid, 16
flout, 311
fluctuation, 91, 92, 93
fluent, 91, 92, 93
flume, 91, 92, 93
fluster, 9
fluvial, 92, 93
flux, 92, 93
foibles, 317
folderol, 19
fontanel, 298
frenetic, 310
fugue, 274, 275, 276
furlong, 179, 180, 182
gadfly, 303
galvanism, 180, 181, 182
gambit, 319
gamut, 15, 184, 187
gargantuan, 186, 187
garret, 199
gauche, 319
gaudy, 6, 9
gazebo, 306

gazette, 200, 205
gecko, 15
gene, 93, 97
genealogy, 95, 97
genial, 94, 97
gentility, 94, 97
gentry, 94, 97
genus, 94, 97
gerrymander, 166, 170, 171
ghee, 16
gherkin, 319
gibe, 21
gimlet, 313
gnome, 20
gnostic, 66, 67
gorgon, 201, 204
gossamer, 201, 205
gourmet, 268, 271
gradation, 100, 101
gradient, 100, 101
gratis, 282, 283
gregarious, 205, 210, 211
guano, 19
guerrilla, 279, 281
guillotine, 184, 187
guinea, 190, 192
halcyon, 194, 197
hauteur, 18
heady, 311
hector, 194, 197, 198
hegemony, 315
hegira, 226, 227, 228
heinous, 21
helot, 241, 242, 243

helpmeet, 195, 197, 198
hermetic, 195, 197, 198
hiatus, 7
hierarchy, 69, 71, 72
hirsute, 22, 317
hobnob, 241, 242, 243
homonym, 48
horde, 185, 187
hoyden, 190, 191, 192
hydrangea, 104, 106
hydrate, 104, 106
hydrophobia, 103, 107
hydroplane, 103, 106
hydroponics, 103, 106
hydropower, 104, 106
hydrosphere, 104, 106
hydrostat, 103, 106
hydrotherapy, 104, 106
icon, 7
iconoclast, 183, 187
idée fixe, 264, 265, 266
ignominious, 154, 155
ignoramus, 66, 67
illegible, 45
illicit, 26
imbibe, 26
imbroglio, 272, 273, 319
imminent, 9
imp, 188, 192
impeccable, 165, 170, 171
impede, 9
impending, 145, 146
implacable, 137, 138
impresario, 272, 273

in toto, 282, 283
inalienable, 51, 52, 53
inane, 315
inanimate, 55, 56, 57
incarcerate, 10
inchoate, 163, 164, 165
incision, 46
inclement, 7
incognito, 65, 67, 272, 273
incredible, 45
incubus, 189, 191, 192
indolence, 189, 192
induce, 81, 83
infidel, 88, 89, 90
influx, 92, 93
innate, 125, 127
inscription, 46
insolent, 193, 197
insouciance, 19
interlocution, 112
interloper, 193, 197
intermezzo, 274, 275, 276
intransigent, 195, 197
inverted, 44
invincible, 45
invoke, 27, 151, 152
irradiate, 27
irreducible, 27
irrelevant, 27
irrevocable, 151, 152
jackanapes, 157, 160, 161
jape, 302
jejune, 15

jeroboam, 157, 160, 161
jitney, 196, 197
jocund, 17
joie de vivre, 264, 265, 266
juggernaut, 182, 187
junket, 196, 197
jurisdiction, 77, 79, 80
juvenilia, 16
kaleidoscope, 188, 192
kibitzer, 260, 261, 262
kiosk, 21, 301
knave, 189, 192
knickers, 198, 204
kowtow, 241, 242, 243
kudos, 255, 256, 257
labyrinth, 173, 174, 175
lackey, 240, 242, 243
lackluster, 7
laconic, 183, 187
lacuna, 256, 257
laissez-faire, 264, 265, 266
lambent, 305
lampoon, 261, 262
languid, 7
lapidary, 313
latent, 6, 9
lavabo, 108, 109, 110
lavage, 108, 109, 110
lemur, 249, 251, 252
lenient, 5
lethargy, 174, 175
liaison, 21
libertine, 186, 187

lingua franca, 18
loath, 17
loqu, 110, 111
loquacious, 7, 112
loqui, 110, 111
lucid, 114, 116, 297
lucubrate, 115, 116
Luddite, 311
luminary, 115, 116
luminous, 115, 116
lyceum, 185, 187
macabre, 19, 185, 187
macadam, 190, 192
Machiavellian, 189, 192
maelstrom, 193, 197
maestro, 275, 276
magenta, 198, 204
magnanimous, 55, 56, 57
mahout, 306
maladjusted, 117, 119, 120
maladroit, 118, 119, 120
malapropism, 118, 119, 120, 297
malediction, 77, 79, 80
malefactor, 117, 119, 120
malevolent, 118, 119, 120
malfeasance, 118, 119, 120
malicious, 118, 119, 120
malign, 119, 120
malignant, 119, 120
mandible, 14
mandrake, 199, 204
manifesto, 272, 273

mantra, 295
martinet, 200, 204
masticated, 297
maternal, 121, 124
matriarch, 69, 71, 72
matriculate, 122, 124
matrilineal, 122, 124
matrix, 122, 124
matron, 121, 124
matronymic, 122, 124
maudlin, 201, 204
mauve, 21
meander, 201, 204
meerschaum, 205, 211
mélange, 313
melée, 267, 268, 270
mendacious, 37
mendicant, 305
mentor, 174, 175
mesa, 279, 281
mesmerize, 166, 169, 171
métier, 319
miasma, 310
mileage, 39
milieu, 264, 265, 266
millennium, 50, 60, 61
minarets, 314
misalliance, 32
misanthrope, 62, 63, 64
misbegotten, 33
miscarriage, 31, 33
misconduct, 81, 83
miscreant, 205, 210, 211
miscue, 32
misericord, 246, 247, 248

mishap, 33
misnomer, 153, 154, 155
monarchy, 69, 70, 72
monotheism, 147, 148, 149
morose, 295
mountebank, 208, 211
muezzin, 313
mugwump, 209, 210, 211
mummery, 318
mustang, 279, 281
muumuu, 248, 251, 252
myriad, 9, 307
nabob, 212, 217
nacre, 18
namby-pamby, 208, 210, 211
narcissism, 216, 217
nascent, 126, 127
natal, 125, 127
nationalism, 126, 127
nativism, 125, 127
nativity, 125, 127
naturalize, 126, 127
necromancy, 313
nee, 126, 127
nefarious, 10
nemesis, 174, 175
nepenthe, 216, 217
nepotism, 217
netsuke, 301
nettlesome, 303
nexus, 302
nihilism, 37
nirvana, 315

noisome, 244, 247, 248
nomenclature, 153, 154, 155
nominal, 154, 155
nominate, 154, 155
nominee, 153, 154, 155
non sequitur, 302
nonce, 302
nonpareil, 301
nonplus, 157, 160, 161
nostrum, 215, 217
noxious, 38
numismatist, 311
obdurate, 17
obeisance, 20
obelisk, 240, 242, 243
obloquy, 111, 112
obsequious, 15
obsequiousness, 10
obtuse, 10
obviates, 11
odium, 282, 283
odoriferous, 45
oeuvre, 318
ogle, 22
oligarchy, 69, 71, 72
olivaceous, 40
ombudsman, 306
ominous, 8
omniscient, 21
opulent, 10
oscillate, 212, 217
ostracize, 176, 180, 182
ottoman, 207, 211

ouija, 244, 247, 248
outré, 311
overcome, 33
overwrought, 32
overzealous, 33
oxymoron, 314
paean, 308, 314
paladin, 241, 242, 243
palatial, 36
palaver, 218, 222, 223
palfrey, 317
panacea, 9, 316
pandemic, 319
pander, 213, 217
panegyric, 319
pannier, 218, 222, 223
pantheism, 147, 148, 149
paralegal, 30
parallel, 30
pariah, 219, 222, 223, 309
parity, 37
parse, 308
parsimonious, 10
partisan, 36
parvenu, 19
pastiche, 309, 311
pastoral, 36
paterfamilias, 130, 132
paternalism, 129, 132
paternoster, 129, 132
pathetic, 49
patio, 277, 278
patois, 308
patriarch, 68, 70, 71
patrician, 128, 132

patrimony, 130, 132
patronage, 129, 132
patronymic, 130, 132
paucity, 309
pecuniary, 219, 222, 223
pedagogue, 213, 217
pedestrians, 36
pedigree, 133, 134, 135
pedometer, 49, 134, 135
peignoir, 319
pejorative, 303
pellucid, 114, 116
pendant, 145, 146
pendulous, 145, 146
penuche, 17
peon, 309
per annum, 58, 60, 61
per se, 282, 283
perfidious, 88, 89, 90
perilous, 37
peroration, 318
perpendicular, 145, 146
petard, 295
phaeton, 209, 211
phantasmagoria, 219, 222, 223
philanderer, 140, 143
philanthropy, 62, 63, 64, 139, 143
philately, 140, 143
philharmonic, 140, 143
philhellene, 141, 143
philodendron, 141, 143
philology, 141, 143
philter, 141, 143

phonograph, 49
piazza, 271, 272, 273
pica, 308
picturesque, 39
piddle, 309
piebald, 308
pimpernel, 308
pince-nez, 19
pinto, 309
pismire, 316
placate, 137, 138, 139
placebo, 137, 138, 309
placid, 136, 138, 139
podiatrist, 133, 135
pompadour, 215, 217
pooh-bah, 317
poplin, 220, 222, 223
poseur, 267, 268, 270
poteen, 308
potpourri, 264, 265, 266
pout, 308
precipitate, 220, 222, 223
precocious, 221, 222, 223
precursor, 26
predatory, 10
predestination, 27
predicate, 77, 79, 80
predictive, 79, 80
prefect, 85, 87
prelapsarian, 318
pretext, 221, 222, 223
prevalent, 7
prevaricate, 163, 164, 165
pro tempore, 282, 283

procrustean, 221, 222, 223
profane, 234, 237, 238
prognosticate, 65, 67
progressive, 100, 101
projectile, 46
proletariat, 223, 227, 228
prolong, 26
Promethean, 238, 242, 243
pronto, 277, 278
prosaic, 6
prosody, 308
protean, 244, 247, 248
protégé, 268, 270
provident, 46
pseudopod, 133, 135, 136
psychotic, 49
pundit, 250, 251, 252
pupa, 309
purge, 9
purloin, 302
pusillanimous, 54, 56
putrefaction, 85, 87
putsch, 14
pygmy, 224, 227, 228
python, 229, 233
quack, 214, 217
quadruped, 133, 135
quagmire, 297
quahog, 243, 247, 248
quintessence, 166, 170, 171
quisling, 158, 160, 161

quixotic, 234, 237, 238
quorum, 239, 242, 243
quotidian, 17
raconteur, 267, 268, 270
ragout, 16
raison d'être, 14
rake, 224, 227, 228
rapport, 264, 265, 266
raze, 298
rebozo, 298
recalcitrant, 230, 232, 233
recanted, 315
recessive, 45
recluse, 46
reductive, 82, 83
reefer, 254, 256, 258
regression, 99, 101
rehabilitate, 9
reincarnation, 27
remonstrate, 303
remora, 231, 232, 233
rendezvous, 264, 265, 266
replica, 272, 273
repulse, 46
requiem, 259, 262
résumé, 263, 265, 266
retrograde, 99, 101
revoke, 151, 152
reynard, 260, 261, 262
rhubarb, 256, 257
rialto, 235, 237, 238
ribald, 15
rigid, 9

rigmarole, 245, 247, 248
Romanesque, 40
rostrum, 249, 252
roustabout, 306
rubicund, 297
rubric, 298
rue, 303
saboteur, 267, 268, 270
salubrious, 14
salver, 235, 237, 238
sanctimonious, 315
sarcophagus, 242, 243, 239
sardonic, 225, 227, 228
satanic, 41
saturnalia, 297
saturnine, 303
savior faire, 319
scapegoat, 261, 262
scarab, 298
schooner, 254, 256, 257
seduce, 82, 83
seer, 306, 311
selfish, 39
sempiternal, 37
sententious, 16
sequel, 45
shibboleth, 236, 237, 238
shoguns, 316
shoji, 19
shrew, 255, 256, 257
sidle, 18
sierra, 279, 281
siesta, 277, 278
silhouette, 230, 233

INDEX OF VOCABULARY WORDS 333

simony, 245, 247, 248
sinecure, 207, 211
sinews, 296
slumgullion, 314
soigné, 311
soiree, 301
solecism, 258, 262
soliloquy, 111, 112
somber, 6
sonata, 274, 275, 276
sophism, 48
sophisticated, 49
sotto voce, 274, 275, 276
spinnaker, 260, 262
spoonerism, 250, 251, 252
status quo, 282, 283
stipend, 144, 145, 146
stoic, 251, 252
succubus, 189
supine, 295
surplice, 246, 247, 248
sybarite, 249, 252
sycophant, 176, 180, 182
syllogism, 30
sylph, 246, 247, 248
synchronize, 48
synchronous, 49
synod, 29
synagogue, 28
syntax, 30
taciturn, 10
tactile, 46
tango, 279, 281
tariff, 259, 262

tartar, 225, 227, 228
tautology, 303
tawdry, 229, 232, 233
termagant, 253, 256, 257
terminate, 45
terra firma, 282, 283
theism, 147, 148, 149
theocracy, 147, 148, 149
theogony, 148, 149
theology, 147, 148, 149
thespian, 235, 237, 238
tiffin, 305
timeless, 39
titanic, 39
toady, 205, 210, 211
tontine, 302
toque, 18
tour de force, 267, 268, 270
tout à fait, 267, 268, 271
tout de suite, 268, 270
tout le monde, 268, 270
traduce, 82, 83
transgress, 99, 101
translucent, 115, 116
treacle, 231, 233
triage, 310
triennial, 58, 60, 61
trumpery, 301
tureen, 307
unanimity, 54, 56
unerring, 33
unfeigned, 33
unkempt, 32
unstable, 45

urchin, 301
uxorious, 305
veracious, 41
verbose, 10
vermicelli, 250, 252
vernacular, 7
viaduct, 81, 83
vicarious, 7
vie, 236, 237
vignette, 16
villanella, 275, 276
viscid, 18

vivacious, 6
vocable, 150, 152
vociferous, 150, 152
waspish, 40
welter, 295
wimple, 295
winsome, 317
wiseacre, 162, 164, 165
wizened, 15
wormwood, 251, 252
yahoo, 250, 251, 252
zealous, 16

INDEX OF ROOTS, PREFIXES, SUFFIXES, AND SPECIAL WORDS

a-, 28, 31
-able, 35
-aceous, 38
ad-, 24
ag, 43
-age, 38
al, 50
-al, 35
all, 50
allo, 50
alter, 50
ami, 42
-an, 35
angel, 289
ann, 57
anthropo, 61
apo-, 28
apron, 289
arch, 68
around the horn, 290
-ate, 34
-ation, 35
BAFO, 289
Baltimore chop, 290
bar, 291
barmy, 292

be-, 31
bean, 286
beef, 286
bellyache, 286
bio, 72
blacklining, 288
blanket, 289
bleed, 288
bloke, 292
blow, 286
bobby, 292
bonnet, 292
boot up, 289
bug off, 286
bugs, 258
cad, 43
call up, 292
can of corn, 290
candy store, 291
cap, 43
cas, 43
CDRL, 289
ced, 43
cept, 43
cess, 43
chemist, 292

chips, 292
chrom, 47
chron, 47
chrono, 47
cid, 43
cir-, 23
cis, 43
clud, 43
clus, 43
com-, 24
conformed copy, 288
cop, 291
cosmo, 47
counterparts, 288
crash, 289
crazy, 291
cred, 43
cum-, 23
cur(r), 43
curs, 43
de-, 24
debug, 289
dem, 47
dictio, 77
dis-, 24
druggist, 291
dummy, 288
-ed, 34
elevator, 291
-en, 35
enn, 57
epi-, 28
-er, 35
-esque, 38
-ette, 34

ex-, 25
fac, 84
fact, 84
fect, 84
fer, 43
-ferous, 39
fid, 87
fide, 87
flu, 90
flunk, 286
French-fried potatoes
    292
fungo, 290
gasoline, 291
gen, 93
geo, 42
gno, 65
grad, 98
grand slam, 290
graphy, 72
gres, 98
gress, 98
gutter, 288
guy, 291
her, 43
hes, 43
hood (of a car), 292
hooked on, 286
hydr(o), 102
-ian, 39
-ic, 38
ice, 289
in-, 25
interface, 289
-ish, 38

-ism, 35
-itis, 38
ject, 43
jig, 289
ladder, 292
laid off, 291
lav, 107
lect, 43
leg, 43
-less, 38
lift, 292
live art, 288
lorry, 292
lu, 107
luc, 114
lum, 114
lux, 114
mackintosh, 292
mal, 117
male, 117
mater, 47, 120, 121
matr, 120, 121
mis-, 31
moola, 286
naked, 292
napkin, 292
nasc, 125
nat, 125
nit, 288
nomen, 153
nomin, 153
on all fours, 288
on-line, 289
onym, 47
-ous, 35

over-, 31
pain in the neck, 286
para-, 28
pater, 128
path, 47
patr, 128
ped, 132
pel(l), 43
pend, 144
petrol, 292
phil, 139
philo, 139
phob, 47
phon, 47
plac, 136
plastered, 286
pod, 132
police officer, 291
pon, 43
port, 43
posit, 43
pre-, 25
pro-, 25
proof, 288
psycho, 47
pub, 292
puls, 43
raincoat, 291
re-, 25
redundant, 292
RFQ, 289
ring up, 292
ripoff, 286
roll size, 288
run (in a stocking), 291

rupt, 43
scrib, 43
script, 43
sect, 43
secut, 44
sens, 43
sent, 43
sequ, 44
serviette, 292
settee, 292
-ship, 39
slush pile, 288
Smokey, 285
sofa, 291
soph, 47, 61
sourpuss, 286
spect, 44
spot, 289
sta, 44
starkers, 292
stat, 44
subway, 291
sweet-shop, 292
syn-, 28

tact, 44
tang, 44
telly, 292
termin, 44
the, 147
theo, 147
tract, 44
truck, 292
TV, 291
-ty, 35
un-, 31
underground, 292
ven, 44
vent, 44
vers, 44
vert, 44
vict, 44
vid, 44
vinc, 44
vis, 44
voc, 150
volut, 44
volv, 44
zap, 286

Notes

Notes